DISCIPLES MAKING DISCIPLES

DISCIPLES MAKING DISCIPLES

A GUIDE FOR COVENANT DISCIPLESHIP GROUPS AND CLASS LEADERS

STEVEN W. MANSKAR

DISCIPLESHIP RESOURCES

ISBNs
978-0-88177-774-1 (print)
978-0-88177-775-8 (mobi)
978-0-88177-776-5 (ePub)

DISCIPLES MAKING DISCIPLES:
COVENANT DISCIPLESHIP WITH ADULTS

Scripture quotations, unless otherwise noted, are from the New Revised Standard Version Bible, copyright © 1989 National Council of Churches of Christ in the United States of America. Used by permission. All rights reserved.

All excerpts and quotations taken from the works of David Lowes Watson as cited are under copyright and are used by permission of Wipf and Stock Publishers. www.wipfandstock.com

Library of Congress Control Number: 2016950116

DR774

This book is dedicated to my mentor and friend

Dr. David Lowes Watson.

His work laid the foundation for everything that follows in the pages of this book.

I give thanks and praise to God for his faithful witness to Jesus Christ and the years of generous teaching, support, and friendship that made my work possible.

CONTENTS

INTRODUCTION

Everyone then who hears these words of mine and acts on them will be like a wise man who built his house on rock. The rain fell, the floods came, and the winds blew and beat on that house, but it did not fall, because it had been founded on rock. And everyone who hears these words of mine and does not act on them will be like a foolish man who built his house on sand. The rain fell, and the floods came, and the winds blew and beat against that house, and it fell—and great was its fall!

—Matthew 7:24-27

This book is a comprehensive guide to the Wesleyan way of forming leaders for discipleship the congregation needs to carry out its mission. Covenant Discipleship groups and class leaders are proven and effective means of forming Christ-centered congregations through training people in the way of Jesus and preparing them to join his mission in the world. Covenant Discipleship groups and class leaders help congregations connect to the solid rock of Christ and his teachings. In Christ-centered congregations members who hear the words of Jesus are equipped to act upon them in joyful obedience, and they in turn lead others to do the same.

The mission of The United Methodist Church is "to make disciples of Jesus Christ for the transformation of the world."[1] The church believes that the local congregation is where disciples are made. Congregations are local outposts of Christ's church. God is worshiped, sacraments are celebrated, and the gospel is proclaimed for the world through the lives and witness of professing Christians. The local congregation is where the church intersects with the world, witnessing to Jesus Christ, introducing seeking people to him, inviting them to quit resisting his grace, and equipping them to join his mission in the world he loves.

How Are Disciples Made?

If disciples are made, then we can say with some certainty that there is a method or process for making them. One does not become a disciple by accident. Making something implies intention and planning. It is a process in which the materials used are shaped or assembled into something new and different. For example, when a factory sets out to make an automobile, it begins with a step-by-step procedure for assembling the parts into a working automobile. The various parts are assembled by the hands and labor of workers with varying levels of expertise and training. At each stage of the process, the work in progress is examined for quality and to make sure that all the parts are assembled properly. Each person involved contributes to the final goal of a car that works dependably and satisfies the customer who will ultimately drive it. Nothing is left to chance. Every step of the manufacturing process is well planned and executed by trained engineers and mechanics.

Making disciples is in some ways similar to making a car. However, this is probably not the best illustration. Such a manufacturing process does not apply well to human beings, because the goal of an assembly line is automobiles that are identical. The first car is the same as the one hundredth car is the same as the one thousandth. The goal of disciple making cannot be to produce people who are identical in belief, practice, and appearance. A more appropriate example for disciple making is that of making pottery. We find this image in scripture:

Yet, O LORD, you are our Father;
>   we are the clay, and you are our potter;
>   we are all the work of your hand. (Isa. 64:8)

So I went down to the potter's house, and there he was working at his wheel. The vessel he was making of clay was spoiled in the potter's hand, and he reworked it into another vessel, as seemed good to him.

Then the word of the LORD came to me: Can I not do with you, O house of Israel, just as this potter has done? says the LORD. Just like the clay in the potter's hand, so are you in my hand, O house of Israel. (Jer. 18:3-6)

The precious children of Zion,
>   worth their weight in fine gold—
how they are reckoned as earthen pots,
>   the work of a potter's hands! (Lam. 4:2)

Has the potter no right over the clay, to make out of the same lump one object for special use and another for ordinary use? (Rom. 9:21)

Like clay in the hand of the potter,
>   to be molded as he pleases,
so all are in the hand of their Maker,
>   to be given whatever he decides. (Sir. 33:13)

The image of potter and clay is appropriate for disciple making because people are like the clay. Each type of clay is different and unique. The potter must know the characteristics of the clay before work begins. The type of clay determines the kind of vessel that can be formed from it. The potter then applies his or her knowledge of the clay and vision for the finished product to shape the clay into the desired vessel. Like the automotive assembly line, however, the potter plans and follows a series of steps that lead to the finished product. The difference is that handmade pieces contain individual characteristics and flaws that make each one unique.

God is the potter who supplies the clay and the vision for the shape and use of the vessel. God also provides the tools necessary for shaping each piece. One tool is the people of the congregation. The people, each of whom God is forming, help form one another. They are, in a way, like the fingers of the potter's hands, shaping, applying pressure, repairing, and guiding the clay into the shape that God seeks for it.

This image, however, presents some problems. First, clay is inanimate. It has no freedom, no choice in what happens to it. In the pottery process the clay is passive. It conforms to whatever shape is imposed upon it. After the clay is dried and baked in the kiln it will remain in the same shape forever. The only way it can change is by breaking into pieces. It can never start over. It cannot grow or change over time. While the image of potter and clay works as a good illustration for disciple making, it is ultimately unsatisfactory.

Yet another, more appropriate, metaphor for disciple making is that of becoming a musician. Listening to music has helped me understand Christian discipleship. I have loved and enjoyed music all my life and have even made efforts at becoming a musician by playing around with my guitar. Listening to music, watching musicians make music, and talking to them have helped me understand that being a disciple of Jesus Christ is very much like being a musician.

Making music, like discipleship, begins with love. People become musicians because they are drawn to and love music. Their love of music attracts them to an instrument—the piano, guitar, horn, violin, or drums. They next must find a teacher who will help them learn how to make music. People learn music from other musicians who are seasoned and who know how to share their gifts with others who want to learn. Like discipleship, music and music making are personal and social.

A person seeking to become a musician very soon learns the importance of study, discipline, and practice. No matter how much natural talent God gives, all musicians understand the necessity of learning and practicing the basics over and over and over again. They know that discipline and practice sets them free to make music to the best of their ability. I know a man who is a gifted trumpet player. He plays with various groups around town and often plays in church worship services. I learned he has been playing the trumpet for over thirty years. He also taught trumpet at a local university. When I asked him, "At this point in your life, how much do you need to practice?" his response helped me understand the link between making music and discipleship. He told me, "I know from experience that if I'm going to play to the best of the ability God has given me, I need to practice at least an hour every day. If I'm preparing for public performance, I need to practice two hours a day." This musician understands that discipline and daily practice set him free to make the music God has given him to play.

Making music, like discipleship, requires listening, discipline, accountability, and support. The purpose of discipline and practice are to prepare the musician for public performance with other musicians. Discipline and practice set the musician free to make the music God has given to him or her.

Jazz is the music that has taught me the most about discipleship, because freedom of expression and improvisation define the musical style. Jazz is often played in a small group. A typical performance begins with the group playing a familiar melody, each person playing his or her part. After two or three times through the song, one of the players begins to improvise on the melody. As he or she plays with the theme, the other members of the band play supporting chords. As each player takes a turn at improvisation, he or she is supported by the band. All this requires skilled listening to one another. This listening and mutual support sets each player free to play with the music and see where it leads them. The goal is to allow the music to take them to new places and new possibilities. All the practice, discipline, listening, and mutual respect for the music, one another, and the audience allow the musicians to get out of the way and let the music play them.

Becoming a disciple of Jesus Christ is very much like becoming a musician. In the waters of baptism God calls us into discipleship. God does not give everyone the gift of making music. However, because we are all created in the image of God, we are all given the same gift: the capacity to give and receive love. The goal of discipleship is to develop this gift to its fullest capacity. Along the way our character, which has been damaged by sin, will be restored to wholeness in the image of Christ. As we grow and mature in loving God with all our heart, soul, mind, and strength and loving our neighbor as ourselves, love becomes a natural response and way of life in the world. As we cooperate with Christ and the Holy Spirit we are equipped to join Christ in his mission of preparing the world for the coming reign of God.

The Baptismal Covenant Shapes the Christian Life

Making disciples, like making musicians, does not happen by accident. It happens with intention born of love for God and love for those whom God loves. The baptismal covenant provides the compass headings for how to make disciples. In it, United Methodist congregations find guidance for developing an intentional process for making disciples of Jesus Christ. Such a system will be immersed in the grace of God from which all of its component parts emerge. The goal is a community whose form and witness in the world are centered on Jesus Christ and devoted to the pursuit of holiness of heart and life.

In this book, I will explore the close relationship between the baptismal covenant and our church's historic "rule of life." "A rule of life is a pattern of spiritual disciplines that provides structure and direction for growth in holiness. . . . It fosters gifts of the Spirit in personal life and human community, helping to form us into the persons God intends us to be."[2] The General Rules of the Methodist Church are the United Methodist *rule of life*.[3] The purpose of the General Rules is to equip Christians to grow in holiness of heart and life through faithfully living the baptismal covenant. Our exploration of forming leaders for discipleship in the congregation will be focused on three questions from the baptismal covenant.[4]

The first question asked of persons to be baptized addresses renunciation, rejection, and repentance of the power and principalities of the world: "Do you renounce the spiritual forces of wickedness, reject the evil powers of this world, and repent of your sin?" The covenant begins by acknowledging the human condition. We admit we are a reflection of the world as it is, broken and ruled by powers and principalities opposed to God and God's reign. We live in this world and are subject to the powers of wickedness and evil that alienate us from God, our neighbors, and ourselves. The world teaches that each of us is the center of the universe, that our individual wants and desires come first. I do not need God or anyone else in my life. My way of life is all about me getting mine by any means necessary. This way of life is what the Bible calls sin. Sin is the way of life opposed to God and God's reign in the world. It leads to behavior that violates God's law of love and justice and does violence to relationships, creation, and ourselves.

In baptism God addresses us as we are. When we stand before the water of the font, we confess that we are sinners in need of redemption. We renounce and reject all that opposes God and his love. We say no to iniquity and evil, and we repent. Repentance means making a 180-degree turn, turning our backs to the old way of sin and turning toward God and life in God's household. Repentance marks the beginning of the healing process. It is the beginning of a new way of life.

In describing the Christian life, the General Rules also begin by acknowledging our sinful human condition when we promise to "continue to evidence our desire for salvation" by "doing no harm by avoiding evil of every kind, especially that which is most generally practiced." The first rule goes on to list behaviors and practices through which people participate in wickedness and evil in the world. The list consists of practices that do harm to persons, relationships, and communities; to their bodies and to their souls. They contribute to alienation from God and one another. Therefore, Christians ought to renounce them and refrain from doing them.

When we evidence our desire for salvation by doing no harm and by avoiding evil of every kind, we witness to the reality and power of God's love and justice in the world. We become participants in God's mission of redeeming this world and setting us free from the powers and principalities of sin and death that demean and destroy life and community. This is the beginning of, and prerequisite for, the formation of holiness of heart and life.

With the first of the General Rules, John Wesley is saying that Christians must stand in the world as people who will not participate in the powers and principalities of the world. He is saying Christians are to be different from the world by resisting the powers of violence, greed, selfishness, individualism, and lust. They do this by refusing to participate in practices that violate the image of God. When Christians resist wickedness and evil, they are witnesses to God's law of love and justice and become agents of healing in a world that is broken and filled with suffering. The baptismal covenant and the General Rules tell us that living as a Christian means accepting the grace we need to acknowledge our own sin and to renounce and resist evil and wickedness in whatever forms they present themselves.

For Christians in the Wesleyan tradition who regularly reaffirm our baptismal covenant, we may respond to the question "Do you renounce the spiritual forces of wickedness, reject the evil powers of this world, and repent of your sin?" by saying, "I do! By doing no harm, by avoiding evil of every kind, especially that which is most generally practiced."

Baptism is deeply personal, but it is not private. It is initiation into the church, which is a community centered in the life and mission of Jesus Christ that promises to "surround *you* with a community of love and forgiveness, that *you* may grow in your trust of God, and be found faithful in *your* service to others." The church also promises to "pray for *you* that *you* may be a true disciple who walks in the way that leads to life." Finally, the congregation promises to "do all in *its* power to increase *your* faith, confirm *your* hope, and perfect *you* in love" (emphasis added). The covenant makes abundantly clear that baptism marks the beginning of a way of life centered in "God's mighty acts of salvation" revealed in the life and mission of Jesus Christ. Baptism, therefore, is both an event that marks us as children of God and members of God's household and a way of life through which we are equipped to participate in Christ's mission of preparing this world for the coming reign of God. The General Rules, therefore, give shape to baptismal living as participants in Christ's mission in the world.

In the second question of the baptismal covenant, the person to be baptized is asked: "Do you accept the freedom and power God gives you to resist evil, injustice, and oppression in whatever forms they present themselves." In the second General Rule, United Methodists "continue to evidence their desire for salvation by doing good; by being in every kind merciful after their power; as they have opportunity, do good of every possible sort, and, as far as possible, to all people: to their bodies . . . [and] to their souls."

When we accept the waters of baptism and our place in God's household, we promise to accept the freedom and power God gives us to resist evil and injustice. Love is the power of God that overcomes evil, injustice, and oppression. Love is God's power that defeats sin by doing good. When we love our neighbor by regular, disciplined practice of acts of compassion and justice, God's love works in and through us. For if we say we love God with all our heart, soul, and mind, then we must therefore love what, and whom, God loves. This means that loving God compels us to love our neighbor as ourselves: "We love because he first loved us. Those who say, 'I love God,' and hate their brothers or sisters, are liars; for those who do not love a brother or sister whom they have seen, cannot love God whom they have not seen. The commandment we have from him is this: those who love God must love their brothers and sisters also" (1 John 4:19-21).

Scripture tells us that our neighbor is anyone anywhere in the world who is hungry, thirsty, sick, imprisoned, or oppressed in any way (Luke 10:29-37). Our neighbor also, according to Jesus, includes those people who are enemies (Matt. 5:43-48). In baptism we are called, and grace empowers us, to love even those who hate us and seek to do us harm. Accepting the freedom and power God gives us to resist evil and injustice means that we will live as agents of compassion and justice in the world that God loves.

When we accept the freedom and power God gives us to resist evil and injustice by doing good to all people, we promise to become advocates and companions with the poor and oppressed peoples of the world. Actively resisting evil and injustice puts us in the company of Jesus, who identifies himself most closely with the victims of the powers and principalities of the world. Jesus said, "Just as you did it to one of the least of these who are members of my family, you did it to me" (Matt. 25:40). When we love our neighbor as ourselves, we reveal the character of our love for Jesus. The grace of God flows through us for the world when we open ourselves to grace through acts of compassion and justice. As grace flows through us, we are able to receive more and more grace that heals and makes us more and more into the persons God created us to be, in the image of Christ.

Jesus told his disciples, you must "love your neighbor as yourself" (Matt. 22:39). The writer of 1 John bluntly states, "Those who say, 'I love God,' and hate their brothers or sisters, are liars" (4:20). The first two baptismal questions quoted above tell us that loving our neighbor requires renouncing wickedness and evil, repentance from sin, and resisting the powers and principalities of the world. The first two General Rules tell us we renounce evil and repent of sin by doing no harm, and doing good in the world is how we resist.

For Christians in the Wesleyan tradition who regularly reaffirm our baptismal covenant, we may respond to the second question, "Do you accept the freedom and power God gives you to resist evil, injustice, and oppression in whatever forms they present themselves?" by also saying, "I do! By doing good, by being in every way merciful as I have opportunity, doing good of every possible sort, and, as far as possible to all people: to their bodies and to their souls."

The third question of the baptismal covenant is "Do you confess Jesus Christ as your Savior, put your whole trust in his grace, and promise to serve him as your Lord, in union with the Church which Christ has opened to people of all ages, nations, and races?" When we respond affirmatively to this question, we claim Jesus Christ as the one whose life, death, and resurrection sets us free from the powers of sin and death. He gives us the freedom to live a new life shaped by his life and teachings. Jesus is Lord of our life. His love sets us free for a lives of "joyful obedience."[5]

When we profess Jesus Christ as Savior and Lord, we promise to take on his way of life, one shaped by the greatest commandment: "You shall love the Lord your God with all your heart, and with all your soul, and with all your mind" (Matt. 22:37). His way is the way of self-giving, self-emptying love described by the apostle Paul in Philippians 2:5-8 and by Charles Wesley in the third stanza of his great hymn "And Can It Be that I Should Gain":

> He left his Father's throne above
> (so free, so infinite his grace!)
> Emptied himself of all but love,
> And bled for Adam's helpless race.
> 'Tis mercy all, immense and free,
> For O my God, it found out me!
> 'Tis mercy all, immense and free,
> For O my God, it found out me!

In Jesus we see that love is the power of God that changes lives and transforms the world. When we are baptized, we take on the life of Christ and begin the training that leads to becoming the person God created us to be, in Christ.

The third baptismal question tells us that living in the world as a Christian is a matrix of relationships. It is first a relationship with Jesus Christ. Second, baptism is a relationship with the church, both the worldwide universal church of Jesus Christ and the local congregation. The church itself is a huge matrix of relationships. There are no solitary Christians. Being a Christian means being part of a community centered in the life and mission of Jesus Christ. While our faith and discipleship are deeply personal, they are not private. We are all responsible for supporting and helping one another to grow and mature in holiness of heart and life.

The third General Rule provides the means for us to nurture both our relationship with God in Christ and with the church. We participate in these relationships "by attending upon all the ordinances of God, such are: the public worship of God; the ministry of the Word, either read or expounded; the Supper of the Lord; family and private prayer; searching the Scriptures; and fasting or abstinence." These are essential practices John Wesley calls "works of piety." They are practices God gives to equip us to participate in the relationship he wants for and with us. These practices nurture our relationships with God and with fellow Christians by opening our hearts and minds to the grace God gives to draw us closer to him and to our neighbor.

An examination of the works of piety reveals that the first three are *acts of worship*, while the second three are *acts of devotion*. Public worship is the most important act of the church, because it tells the world we are a people centered in God who is revealed in the life, death, and resurrection of Jesus Christ. We proclaim that Christ is the Lord of the universe and he is at work redeeming the world, preparing it for the coming reign of God. In worship we offer ourselves to the service of God and to building one another up in holiness of heart and life.

We are people of the word that is read in the holy scriptures, proclaimed in preaching, prayer, and lived through mission in the world. In the Lord's Supper Christ invites us to his table, where he forgives our sins and sets us free for joyful obedience and service with his mission in the world. At the table we take his body and blood into our bodies, and then he sends us into the world to serve as witnesses to his love and justice. Through praise, prayer, word, and sacrament the church becomes a sign and foretaste of God's reign on earth as it is in heaven. When we participate in these practices our hearts are opened to the grace Christ gives us. We all need his grace if we are to live as fully human beings and channels of God's love for the world.

Personal and family prayer, searching the scriptures, and fasting or abstinence are acts of devotion done in private. They are how we open ourselves to God and the grace he wants to give us. All relationships require regular, intimate communication. Prayer is the primary means of communication with God. It is where God promises to meet us. All we need to do is show up and keep our daily appointment with him.

Searching the scriptures is how we learn God's story and our place in it. It is where we learn the good news of God's kingdom and how to live as faithful ambassadors for and citizens in that kingdom.

Fasting or abstinence are important because they are how we imitate Christ's self-emptying love for the world. When we empty ourselves we are reminded that God is God and we are not. When we feel the discomfort in our bellies after skipping a meal, we remember that we are not self-sufficient; that we depend upon the fruit of God's creation to live. Fasting opens the heart to God and those whom God loves, especially the poor and hungry people of the world. That is why fasting is always accompanied by prayer.

For Christians in the Wesleyan tradition who regularly reaffirm our baptismal covenant, we may respond to the question "Do you confess Jesus Christ as your Savior, put your whole trust in his grace, and promise to serve him as your Lord, in union with the church which Christ has opened to people of all ages, nations, and races?" by saying: "I do! By practicing all the ordinances of God: the public worship of God, the ministry of the Word, the Lord's Supper, family and private prayer, searching the Scriptures, and fasting or abstinence."

The baptismal covenant describes the threefold relationship between God, the baptized person, and the church. The General Rules provide simple and practical guidance for how to live, grow, and thrive in those relationships. They lead us toward the goal of life in God's household, which is holiness of heart and life, inward love of God with all our heart, soul, and mind lived out in the world by self-giving love of all that God loves.

Who Is a Disciple?

The English word *disciple* is derived from the Latin *discipulus*, meaning "a learner or pupil; one who accepts and follows a given doctrine or teacher."[6] A disciple of Jesus Christ, therefore, is a person who accepts and follows his teachings. All who are baptized in the name of the triune God and confess Jesus Christ as Savior and Lord are Christians and, by definition, disciples.

Our Wesleyan tradition gives some further help answering the question, who is a disciple? A disciple is a person who has faith in Christ, and their faith bears fruit through following the General Rules: by doing no harm, by avoiding evil, by doing good to all as often as possible, and by practicing the instituted means of grace (worship, the Lord's Supper, listening to scripture read and expounded, personal and family prayer, Bible study, and fasting or abstinence). Christian faith is revealed by a life that pursues holiness of heart and life, which is universal love filling the heart and governing the life and having the mind that was in Christ, and to walk just as he walked (Phil. 2:5; 1 John 2:6).

A disciple's life is shaped by "faith working through love" (Gal. 5:6). A disciple's life pursues wholehearted love of God through self-giving service in the world, especially among people who are poor, sick, prisoners, lonely, tired, and lost (see Matt. 22:37-39; 25:31-46).

The General Rules are for all Christians. They are a simple guide for living the Christian life in the world. They help Christians to be mindful of the basics of loving God, loving neighbors, and loving one another. They help disciples follow all the teachings of Jesus and not only those that suit their temperament. A disciple, therefore, is a Christian who does his or her best to follow Jesus and his teachings every day of the week.

Two Kinds of Disciples

John Wesley provides some assistance for identifying types of discipleship in his sermon "The More Excellent Way." Here he reflects on the nature of Christian discipleship. He acknowledges a long-held belief that there are two kinds of Christians:

> The one lived an innocent life, conforming in all things not sinful to the customs and fashions of the world, doing many

good works, abstaining from gross evils, and attending the ordinances of God. They endeavoured in general to have a conscience void of offence in their outward behaviour, but did not aim at any particular strictness, being in most things like their neighbours. The other sort of Christians not only abstained from all appearance of evil, were zealous of good works in every kind, and attended all the ordinances of God; but likewise used all diligence to attain the whole mind that was in Christ, and laboured to walk in every point as their beloved Master. In order to this they walked in a constant course of universal self-denial, trampling on every pleasure which they were not divinely conscious prepared them for taking pleasure in God. They took up their cross daily. They strove, they agonized without intermission, to enter in at the strait gate. This one thing they did; they spared no pains to arrive at the summit of Christian holiness: "leaving the first principles of the doctrine of Christ, to go on to perfection"; "to know all that love of God which passeth knowledge, and to be filled with all the fullness of God."[7]

The first group Wesley describes comprises the vast majority of Christians. They attend worship in varying degrees of frequency, give money to the church, may attend a Sunday school class, send their children to Sunday school, and do their best to be good, hardworking, loving people. Their appearance and behavior is virtually indistinguishable from that of their non-Christian and nonreligious neighbors.

The second kind of Christian described by Wesley are those women and men who have made an intentional, deeply personal commitment to following and serving Jesus Christ in the world through joyful obedience to his commandments. They are disciplined in practicing the means of grace, both the works of piety and the works of mercy. These disciples are deeply committed to Christ and pursue a way of life that leads to holiness of heart and life.

Wesley is very clear in this sermon to say that both groups are equally saved by grace through faith (Eph. 2:8). Each is following

Christ in the way that best suits them. That being said, Wesley also asserts that the community of faith and its leaders are responsible for encouraging and equipping the first type of Christian to desire to mature and move toward the second: "I would be far from quenching the smoking flax, from discouraging those that serve God in a low degree. But I would not wish them to stop here: I would encourage them to come up higher, without thundering hell and damnation in their ears, without condemning the way wherein they were, telling them it is the way that leads to destruction. I will endeavour to point out to them what is in every respect a more excellent way."[8] He wants them to know that there is more to Christian discipleship and that God wants them to become more fully the persons God created them to be. The "more excellent way" is the way of self-giving, self-emptying love that leads to holiness of heart and life, to have the mind of Christ (Phil. 2:5), and "to walk just as he walked" (1 John 2:6).

The Apostles and the Crowd

Scripture supports this two-tiered discipleship. We find it in the Gospel accounts of Jesus and his relationship with the disciples and the crowd. One of the clearest examples is found in the accounts of Jesus feeding the five thousand. Look, for example, at Mark 6:30-44:

> The apostles gathered around Jesus, and told him all that they had done and taught. He said to them, "Come away to a deserted place all by yourselves and rest a while." For many were coming and going, and they had no leisure even to eat. And they went away in the boat to a deserted place by themselves. Now many saw them going and recognized them, and they hurried there on foot from all the towns and arrived ahead of them. As he went ashore, he saw a great crowd; and he had compassion for them, because they were like sheep without a shepherd; and he began to teach them many things. When it grew late, his disciples came to him and said, "This

is a deserted place, and the hour is now very late; send them away so that they may go into the surrounding country and villages and buy something for themselves to eat." But he answered them, "You give them something to eat." They said to him, "Are we to go and buy two hundred denarii worth of bread, and give it to them to eat?" And he said to them, "How many loaves have you? Go and see." When they had found out, they said, "Five, and two fish." Then he ordered them to get all the people to sit down in groups on the green grass. So they sat down in groups of hundreds and of fifties. Taking the five loaves and the two fish, he looked up to heaven, and blessed and broke the loaves, and gave them to his disciples to set before the people; and he divided the two fish among them all. And all ate and were filled; and they took up twelve baskets full of broken pieces and of the fish. Those who had eaten the loaves numbered five thousand men.

We see in this story the two types of Christians. The first is represented by the crowd of people who were drawn to Jesus and his disciples. They came to be healed and to hear the good news of the kingdom of God. They needed to hear the good news that sins are forgiven, that God loves them, that God will give them the faith needed to heal them (body, mind, spirit, and relationship). Jesus has compassion on them. He gives them all that he has to offer. They came to him with an emptiness in their lives that the world cannot fill. Only Jesus can satisfy their longing for hope, healing, and meaning in their lives.

The apostles represent the second type of Christians. They are the ones who committed their lives to walking with, following, and serving with Jesus in the world. They are also the disciples whom Jesus equips to feed, care for, and heal the crowd. Jesus takes what they have and multiplies it to meet the needs of the others who come for healing and forgiveness of sins and to hear the good news of the reign of God.

Baptized and Professing Christians

This two-tiered model of discipleship is also found in our under-standing of baptism and church membership. We have two types of membership in The United Methodist Church: baptized and profess-ing. The roll of the baptized contains all persons who have received the sacrament of baptism. God has marked them as his own children and welcomed them into God's household, the church. The church, in turn, promises to "surround these persons with a community of love and forgiveness." It promises to do all in its power to increase their faith, confirm their hope, and perfect them in love.

The professing members are baptized Christians who have accepted God's gifts of forgiveness, acceptance, and faith. They promise to follow and serve Christ in the world as his faithful dis-ciples and to support the ministries of the church through their prayers, presence, gifts, service, and witness. The expectation is that professing members are regularly present and participating in wor-ship, Bible study, and other ministries of the congregation. Ideally, they are in a small group with other professing members for mutual support and accountability in following and witnessing to Jesus Christ in the world.

The mission of the church, of course, is to welcome all people who are seeking a relationship with God through Jesus Christ, to intentionally nurture them in faith, and to help them pursue holiness of heart and life. The congregation promises to do this every time persons are baptized or confirmed and the pastor delivers the Com-mendation and Welcome: "I commend these persons to your love and care. Do all in your power to increase their faith, confirm their hope, and perfect them in love." Paragraph 220 in *The Book of Discipline of The United Methodist Church, 2012* describes how congregations are to help members become disciples of Jesus Christ by keeping their baptismal promises:

> *The Call to Ministry of All the Baptized*—All members of Christ's universal church are called to share in the minis-try which is committed to the whole church of Jesus Christ.

Therefore, each member of The United Methodist Church is to be a servant of Christ on mission in the local and world-wide community. This servanthood is performed in family life, daily work, recreation and social activities, responsible citizenship, the stewardship of property and accumulated resources, the issues of corporate life, and all attitudes toward other persons. Participation in disciplined groups such as covenant discipleship groups or class meetings is an expected part of personal mission involvement. Each member is called upon to be a witness for Christ in the world, a light and leaven in society, and a reconciler in a culture of conflict. Each member is to identify with the agony and suffering of the world and to radiate and exemplify the Christ of hope. The standards of attitude and conduct set forth in the Social Principles (Part V) shall be considered as an essential resource for guiding each member of the Church in being a servant of Christ on mission.

Covenant Discipleship Groups and Class Leaders

Covenant Discipleship groups and class leaders provide the foundation needed for a congregation to live out its mission of making disciples of Jesus Christ for the transformation of the world.[9] The mission of Covenant Discipleship groups and class leaders is to form the leaders in discipleship the congregation needs to faithfully carry out its mission.

Leadership in the Methodist tradition is historically a partnership between laity and clergy. In the early nineteenth century, Methodism experienced rapid growth. Most clergy served several congregations spread across large geographic areas known as circuits. They were known as circuit riders, because they traveled on horseback from congregation to congregation. They typically arrived in each congregation once every three months.

During the weeks and months the ordained pastor was absent, the pastoral ministry of discipling the people of the church was done by laypersons known as class leaders. Methodists were required to meet weekly in small groups known as classes. A class consisted of twelve to fifteen people led by a member of the congregation whom the pastor and congregation acknowledged to be a leader in discipleship. They worked as pastoral partners with the ordained, appointed circuit rider.

The system of class meetings and the pastoral leadership provided by class leaders freed the circuit riders to itinerate and plant new congregations. The focus on discipleship and mission led to rapid growth and congregational vitality. Methodism is at its best when clergy and laity work alongside each other as partners in the mission to make disciples of Jesus Christ for the transformation of the world.

Where are class leaders to be found today? They are the women and men who are ready and willing to be intentional and accountable for their discipleship. They are Christians who are seeking to live in the world as disciples of Jesus Christ.

Covenant Discipleship groups are designed for such persons. Some members of Covenant Discipleship groups will answer God's call to serve as class leaders. Class leaders work alongside the appointed pastor as discipleship coaches. They are given a class of up to twenty members of the congregation who desire to live as disciples of Jesus Christ. Each class is a missional unit of the congregation. The class leader's job is to help members of his or her class live and grow as faithful disciples of Jesus Christ and be shaped by the General Rule of Discipleship: "To witness to Jesus Christ in the world and to follow his teachings through acts of compassion, justice, worship, and devotion under the guidance of the Holy Spirit."[10] They do this through regular contact with class members via personal visits, telephone, e-mail, and social media.

Retraditioning classes and, in particular, the office of class leader will go a long way to help United Methodist congregations grow in vitality. The church's task is to equip and deploy the laypersons whom God is calling to make disciples among the people of their home congregations and communities. By commissioning them to serve as class leaders and discipleship coaches, the church recognizes and affirms their call and is faithful to its mission to make disciples of Jesus Christ for the transformation of the world.

> Help us to help each other, Lord,
> Each other's cross to bear;
> Let each his friendly aid afford,
> And feel his brother's care.

> Help us to build each other up,
> Our little stock improve;
> Increase our faith, confirm our hope,
> And perfect us in love.[11]

Conclusion

A disciple is a Christian who has been baptized in the name of the triune God and welcomed into the fellowship of the church. A disciple is a Christian who comes to the Lord's Table with open heart and hands, receives Christ's body and blood, and is sent into the world to serve as an agent of God's love and justice.

A disciple believes the ancient prayer that says "to know Christ is eternal life and to serve Christ is perfect freedom."[12] Disciples renounce the spiritual forces of wickedness, reject the evil powers of this world, and repent of their sins. They accept the freedom and power God gives them to resist evil, injustice, and oppression in whatever forms they encounter. And, they confess Jesus Christ as their Savior, put their whole trust in his grace, and promise to serve him as their Lord, in union with the church, which Christ has opened to people of all ages, nations, and races.

Discipleship is a journey. It is a deeply personal experience of self-discovery, struggle, service, and growth. While it is personal, the journey of discipleship is not private. Disciples do not walk alone with Christ. They walk with Jesus and the others he chooses for them (see John 15:16). Some are more seasoned, while others are seekers. Christ brings people together to train them in his way of life. As they become more and more Christlike for each other, they *become* able to love their neighbors in the world. The writer of the Gospel according to John puts it this way: "To all who received [Christ], who believed in his name, he gave power to become children of God, who were born, not of blood or of the will of the flesh or of the will of man, but of God" (1:12-13). The journey of discipleship, therefore, is a process of *becoming* the human beings God created us to be; fully human in the image of Christ and a channel of grace for the healing and redemption of planet earth.

The journey of discipleship has a goal. The Wesleyan tradition believes the goal is "perfection in love" (1 John 4:18), "holiness of heart and life," and "to have the mind of Christ and to walk just as he walked."[13] Disciples of Jesus Christ take responsibility for one another as they obey his commandment to "love one another. Just as I have loved you. . . . By this everyone will know that you are my disciples" (John 13:34-35). Jesus gives his disciples the grace they need to hear his words and put them into action.

What does this "perfection in love" look like? Paul describes the marks of Christian maturity in Galatians 5:22-23, "The fruit of the Spirit is love, joy, peace, patience, kindness, generosity, faithfulness, gentleness, and self-control," and Colossians 3:12-17:

> As God's chosen ones, holy and beloved, clothe your-selves with compassion, kindness, humility, meekness, and patience. Bear with one another and, if anyone has a com-plaint against another, forgive each other; just as the Lord has forgiven you, so you also must forgive. Above all, clothe yourselves with love, which binds everything together in per-fect harmony. And let the peace of Christ rule in your hearts, to which indeed you were called in the one body. And be thankful. Let the word of Christ dwell in you richly; teach and admonish one another in all wisdom; and with grati-tude in your hearts sing psalms, hymns, and spiritual songs to God. And whatever you do, in word or deed, do every-thing in the name of the Lord Jesus, giving thanks to God the Father through him.

All this is God's gift and work in, with, and for those who desire to be and live as disciples of Jesus Christ by the power of the Holy Spirit. The disciple's task is to participate and cooperate with the work that God is doing and promises to do through power of the Holy Spirit.

Finally, a disciple is a person who strives to live into the Covenant Prayer. Although few are there yet, all are seeking and running toward the goal, with much love and support, trusting in the grace that God gives to all through faith in Jesus Christ by the power of the Holy Spirit:

> I am no longer my own, but thine.
> Put me to what thou wilt, rank me with whom thou wilt.
> Put me to doing, put me to suffering.
> Let me be employed by thee or laid aside for thee,
> exalted for thee or brought low for thee.
> Let me have all things, let me have nothing.
> I freely and heartily yield all things
> to thy pleasure and disposal.
> And not, O glorious and blessed God,
> Father, Son, and Holy Spirit,
> thou art mine, and I am thine. So be it.
> And the covenant which I have made on earth,
> let it be ratified in heaven. Amen.[14]

Now is the time for United Methodist congregations to rediscover and retradition the disciple-making ministry of the class leader. Experience and tradition tell us that disciples make disciples. The Wesleyan tradition provides us with a proven and effective method for disciple making in the twenty-first century.

This is where God's mystery involves the people who call themselves Christians. It is strange indeed that God should have chosen as colleagues in these daring acts of salvation a community of people known as the church. Their part in the drama is limited, but it is critical. They have been entrusted with the singular task of letting the people of the world know what God has done and is doing to redeem their planet; and they have been gifted with the firstfruits of God's salvation in their life and work. But they are very ordinary people, these church folk, and much of the time they are barely competent for their task. It is deeply mysterious, to them and to the rest of the world, why they should have been chosen for such important work.

If Christians are to understand their role, therefore, and undertake their task with integrity, they must not evade the mysteries of God's salvation; nor must they try to resolve them. Christians must rather seek to join with the risen Christ *in the midst of* the mysteries, proclaiming the hope of the gospel. They must work faithfully in the world, waiting expectantly for God's redemption to be fulfilled, and wrestling with the tensions of a message which points to the future. To do all of this, they must be centered on Christ, empowered by the Holy Spirit; and they must be formed into faithful, obedient disciples. Nothing less will suffice.

—David Lowes Watson
Forming Christian Disciples, pp. 4–5

CHAPTER 1

Congregational Purpose and Mission

Everyone then who hears these words of mine and acts on them will be like a wise man who built his house on rock. The rain fell, the floods came, and the winds blew and beat on that house, but it did not fall, because it had been founded on rock. And everyone who hears these words of mine and does not act on them will be like a foolish man who built his house on sand. The rain fell, and the floods came, and the winds blew and beat against that house, and it fell—and great was its fall!

—Matthew 7:24-27

Who, or what, is at the center of your congregation? Who, or what, drives and motivates the congregation's life and activities? Where does the congregation focus its energy? What is the congregation passionate about?

These are questions about purpose and mission. Purpose is the reason for the congregation's life and activity. It is the why of a congregation's existence. The purpose motivates the activities and determines how resources are used. The best way to determine a congregation's purpose is to look at where and how it allocates its resources and energy.

Mission is different from purpose. The word *mission* is derived from the Latin word *missio*, which means "sent." A congregation's mission determines the impact it has in the local community and the world. It is what the congregation does to touch the lives of people living in its neighborhood. Mission is what the congregation does to communicate its purpose in the community and the world.

Purpose and Mission in Four Types of Congregations[1]

When its purpose is providing for and building the membership, *a congregation is church centered*. The mission of these congregations is focused on the membership, staff, and building. One could say the mission of a church-centered congregation is the church itself. Resources, activities, and energy are all directed toward the purpose of meeting members' social, emotional, and spiritual needs. The mission is focused on increasing the number of members through programming and marketing.

When members join the church, they learn of the benefits and services they can expect from staff and lay leaders. People join expecting their social and emotional needs will be met through the various programs and activities offered by the staff. The primary purpose of participation in service in the community or abroad is personal growth and blessing. The purpose and mission of the church aim to increase happiness and emotional and spiritual health among its members.

The evangelism committee recruits new members. This is done through advertising and members inviting friends and neighbors. People are invited to come and experience the great worship service, welcoming community, and the many ways they will personally benefit by joining.

The people of the congregation are the focus of a church-centered congregation. Following Christ and the gospel are programs for people who may be interested in discipleship. The time and energy of clergy and staff are consumed by serving the emotional and social needs of members. Very little of their time is devoted to serving outside the church.

The *program-centered congregation* is similar to the church-centered congregation. Both emphasize the benefit of personal growth that comes with membership. Staff time is consumed by serving members and their needs. And mission is focused on increasing church membership.

The purpose of a program-centered congregation is providing quality programs to meet members' emotional, social, and spiritual needs. Paid clergy and staff organize the programs with a team of dedicated laypersons who lead and teach the various program offerings. Programs are developed by staff or purchased from denominational and other publishing companies. The selected programs serve all ages, from preschool children and youth to older adults. The goal is to provide a varied menu of options to attract and keep as many members as possible.

The key characteristics of a program are these:

- It has a beginning and an end point. Most programs run from four to eight sessions. Some may be as long as thirty-four weeks, but the vast majority tend to be fewer than twelve weeks or sessions.
- It is guided by a curriculum that includes a leader and participant guide. Some may include a video featuring a popular author or scholar who address the topic at hand.
- Most programs aim to increase knowledge on a particular topic or practice of Christian faith or of other faith traditions.

In a program-centered congregation, discipleship may be one program offering among many. Worship is another program for all members to participate in as often as possible; it is the one program that is ongoing. Programmatic worship tends to feature four- to twelve-week sermon series that emphasize various themes and topics throughout the year. Worship is seen as a technique for attracting people to the church and keeping them engaged.

With programs at the center, these congregations offer Christ and the gospel to those who are interested in discipleship and mission. Programs are presented as ways of learning about God, Christ, the gospel and how to live a better life. They convey information and knowledge of the Bible, theology, and social issuues but rarely lead to changed hearts.

Another form of congregation is *pastor centered*, typically one that has a dynamic, winsome, highly effective pastor. People are drawn to the church by the personality and preaching of the pastor. Such congregations are shaped by the pastor's personal preferences, interpretation of scripture, theology, and practice of ministry.

The church desperately needs gifted pastors who are effective preachers, organizers, and leaders. But they need to communicate clearly to the congregation that members are following Jesus Christ and his mission in the world. The pastor is responsible for always pointing the people toward following the one who is Lord and Savior of the world, and not to himself or herself.

This is not to condemn strong, effective pastoral leaders but to say that when pastors become the center of the congregation, they tend to make disciples of themselves rather than disciples of Jesus Christ. When such pastors are removed, either by moving on to another congregation, or due to retirement, or because of misbehavior, the congregation suffers. Members who were attracted by and devoted to the pastor often leave when he or she departs. A leadership vacuum remains, because Christ and his mission were placed at the margins by the power of the pastor's personality and leadership skill.

Christ-centered congregations keep Jesus Christ at the center of purpose and mission. The church, programs, and pastors work together to equip members for joining Christ in his mission in the world. Congregational life is organized to help members keep the promises they have made in the baptismal covenant. Clergy and laity understand that baptism is initiation into the church as God's household, and that members are responsible to "do all in [our] power to increase their faith, confirm their hope, and perfect them in love."[2] This means the church's life, programs, and pastoral leaders all work together to help everyone serve and witness to Jesus Christ and his mission in the world.

In Matthew 7:24-27, quoted at the beginning of the chapter, Jesus speaks about two kinds of houses. One is built on the solid foundation of stone. The other is built upon sand. The house built on stone is the people who hear and act upon his words. That house is able to withstand the flood and storms of the world. The ones who hear Jesus' words and do not obey his teachings are like a house built on sand. Because they lack a solid foundation they will be washed away by the storm.

Jesus' teachings are the solid foundation of God's word. Jesus tells his disciples, "I am the way, and the truth, and the life" (John 14:6). Jesus and his teaching are unchanging and reliable. They are like stone that supports the house capable of withstanding the flood. The way, truth, and life of God do not change with the times. They are eternal, for all times and all people.

Scripture tells us the church is not the building in which the congregation gathers. The church is the community centered in the life and mission of Jesus Christ. The apostle Paul uses organic metaphors to describe the nature of the church: a living, breathing, walking, and witnessing "body of Christ" in the world. He also uses the metaphor of the church as the "household of God" built upon the foundation of the apostles and prophets, with Christ as the cornerstone: "So then you are no longer strangers and aliens, but you are citizens with the saints and also members of the household of God, built upon the foundation of the apostles and prophets, with Christ Jesus himself as the cornerstone. In him the whole structure is joined together and grows into a holy temple in the Lord; in whom you also are built together spiritually into a dwelling place for God" (Eph. 2:19-22). Such an image harkens back to Jesus' referring to himself as the temple that will be destroyed and raised up after three days (John 2:19).

Covenant Discipleship Groups for Christ-Centered Congregations

Covenant Discipleship groups are part of the foundation of Christ-centered congregations. Obedience to Jesus' teachings is essential to keeping the purpose and mission focused on him and not the latest cultural trends. The people who participate in the groups are the ones who hear and act upon Jesus' teachings, summarized by him in Matthew 22:37-39: " 'You shall love the Lord your God with all your heart, and with all your soul, and with all your mind.' This is the greatest and first commandment. And a second is like it: 'You shall love your neighbor as yourself.' " Covenant Discipleship groups form the leaders in discipleship every congregation needs to faithfully obey Jesus' commission to "go therefore and make disciples of all nations, baptizing them in the name of the Father and of the Son and of the Holy Spirit, and teaching them to obey everything that I have commanded you. And remember, I am with you always, to the end of the age" (Matt. 28:19-20).

The process of weekly mutual accountability and support for following and witnessing to Jesus in the world, guided by a covenant shaped by the General Rule of Discipleship ("To witness to Jesus Christ in the world and to follow his teachings through acts of compassion, justice, worship, and devotion under the guidance of the Holy Spirit"[3]), helps members grow in holiness of heart and life. Habitual practice of acts of compassion, justice, worship, and devotion opens the heart and mind to Christ's love for the world. Daily practice and weekly accountability forms persons more and more into the women and men God created them to be. They are equipped to serve as small group leaders, Bible study leaders, and class leaders; they are the disciples who disciple others in the congregation and in the world.

Jesus tells us in Luke 6:46-49 that discipleship is the foundation of the church. Discipleship is knowing, listening, learning, and obeying Jesus. Mike Breen, in his excellent book *Building a Discipling Culture*, writes:

> If you make disciples, you always get the church. But if you make a church, you rarely get disciples. . . .
>
> Effective discipleship builds the church, not the other way around. We need to understand the church as the effect of discipleship and not the cause. If you set out to build the church, there is no guarantee you will make disciples. It is far more likely that you will create consumers who depend on the spiritual services that religious professionals provide.[4]

Covenant Discipleship groups serve as an essential part of disciple-making process that must be the foundation upon which a congregation is built. Other parts of such a foundation are shared pastoral leadership, catechesis (Christian teaching with formation), evangelism, and stewardship. Such a foundation leads a congregation to live and serve as a community that listens to and acts upon the words of Jesus.

The mission of Covenant Discipleship groups is to form leaders in discipleship whom the congregation needs to faithfully live out its mission: to make disciples of Jesus Christ for the transformation of the world.

God's Mission Needs God's People

When Jesus began his public ministry, he immediately gathered a small group of followers to join him in his mission proclaiming the good news of God's reign on earth as in heaven (see Matt. 10:1-15; Mark 3:13-19; Luke 6:12-16; John 1:35-51). Jesus knew that he could not accomplish his mission alone. God's mission requires the cooperation and participation of God's people. Jesus gathered a team of devoted followers to help him spread the good news of God's reign. He trained them in God's way of love and justice so that they could continue the work after his death and resurrection.

A good example of the way Jesus prepared the disciples for their work is the feeding of the five thousand (Matt. 14:13-21; Mark 6:30-44; Luke 9:10-17; John 6:1-14). After an intense time of preaching and healing, Jesus and the twelve get away for some downtime. But the crowd gets word of where they are going and is waiting when they arrive. Jesus does not send the people away. He immediately gets to work healing and teaching, giving them what they need. The disciples observe Jesus ministering to the people's needs. One of them goes to him late in the day to encourage Jesus to send the crowd away so they can go find dinner for themselves. But Jesus tells the disciples they should feed the crowd. To which the disciples reply, "We have nothing here but five loaves and two fish" (Matt. 14:17). Jesus instructs them to have the crowd sit down in groups of fifty. He then tells the disciples to give him the bread and fish. As he took the food, "he looked up to heaven, and blessed and broke the loaves, and gave them to the disciples, and the disciples gave them to the crowds" (Matt. 14:19b). To their amazement, everyone had plenty to eat. Afterward, the disciples collected twelve baskets filled with leftovers.

Jesus called the twelve into relationship with him. Through teaching and example he showed them how to live and love as God loves. The crowd came to Jesus for many reasons. Some were sick and needed healing. Some were blind, disabled, or deaf. Some were searching for meaning and hope for their lives. Some wanted to hear the good news of God's kingdom. Some were simply curious. And some were looking for a reason to discredit and destroy Jesus and his mission. Jesus met and accepted people as they were. He had compassion on them, healed them, and expected nothing from them.

When the disciples insisted Jesus send the crowd away to find dinner, he told them they had everything they needed to provide for the crowd's hunger. All they had to do was give him what they had and he would make it more than enough. What did they have? Besides the five loaves and two fish, the disciples had their relationship with Jesus. His grace was sufficient, in abundance, to equip them to serve the people who came to Jesus.

When disciples give themselves, their gifts, and their talents to Jesus, he is able to empower them to be living witnesses to God's kingdom of love and justice. His grace equips them to join his mission in the world. Jesus makes this explicit in John 15:1-5: "I am the true vine, and my Father is the vinegrower. He removes every branch in me that bears no fruit. Every branch that bears fruit he prunes to make it bear more fruit. You have already been cleansed by the word that I have spoken to you. Abide in me as I abide in you. Just as the branch cannot bear fruit by itself unless it abides in the vine, neither can you unless you abide in me. I am the vine, you are the branches. Those who abide in me and I in them bear much fruit, because apart from me you can do nothing."

Discipleship is connection with Jesus. Disciples are like the branches of a grapevine. Their purpose is to bear fruit. They are able to bear fruit only as long as they are connected to the vine, which is Jesus. He supplies all that is necessary to produce the fruit. He tends the branches to help them be what they were created for. Love is the fruit of discipleship.

Branches depend upon one another to grow and bear fruit. When we look at a grapevine, we notice that the branches are intertwined with each other. Seeing where one begins and another ends is difficult. There are no solitary branches, just as there are no solitary Christians. Which is why we are baptized into the community of the church, which promises to surround us with love and forgiveness, to pray for us, and to help us live and serve with Christ that we may become the persons God created us to be.

The examples of Jesus calling the twelve and the parable of the vine and branches tell us that disciples are made in community through relationships of mutual love, accountability, and support. Jesus initiates the relationship and helps the person grow in holiness through teaching and example. He called twelve ordinary men and mentored them into holiness of heart and life by showing them how to live as citizens in God's kingdom. They learned how to live his way of life by observing and imitating his example.

Discipleship Incubators: Early Methodist Societies

John Wesley learned from scripture, tradition, reason, and experience that Jesus' way is the most effective disciple-making process. He organized the Methodist societies to reconstitute the disciple-making practices of the early church. Wesley wrote in the preface to the first collection of hymns he and his brother Charles published in 1739, "The gospel of Christ knows of no religion, but social; no holiness but social holiness." He knew that people become followers of Jesus when they join others who are following him. They come to know Jesus through the relationships formed in Christian community.

Wesley organized the societies to be incubators of discipleship. The goal was to teach people how to live the Christian life and to provide the ongoing loving support and accountability needed to live and love the Jesus way. Wesley understood that people change when they are shown how to live. When they joined a Methodist society, people were not given a book to study and discuss. They were initiated into the basic practices of discipleship described for them in the General Rules:

> It is therefore expected of all who continue therein that they should continue to evidence their desire of salvation:
> *First*: By doing no harm, by avoiding evil of every kind, especially that which is most generally practiced, . . .
> *Secondly*: By doing good; by being in every kind merciful after their power; as they have opportunity, doing good of every possible sort, and, as far as possible, to all men . . .
> *Thirdly*: By attending upon all the ordinances of God; such are:
> The public worship of God; the ministry of the Word, either read or expounded; the Supper of the Lord; family and private prayer; searching the Scriptures; fasting or abstinence.[5]

The General Rules were devised by Wesley in 1742 after he observed a lack of Christian discipline among the Methodist societies in Newcastle upon Tyne, England. He realized they lacked discipline because they had no rule to guide them in the Christian life. Wesley recognized they needed a rule of life similar to those used by monastic communities. Historians today believe the Methodist movement is very similar to the Franciscan monastic movement

organized around the life and teachings St. Francis of Assisi. The
Methodists and Franciscans share similar concern for ministry with
the poor and care for all creation.

The General Rules provided the Methodists with the set of
basic practices that helped them to obey the teachings of Jesus. He
described the expectations of discipleship in Luke 9:23: "If any want
to become my followers, let them deny themselves and take up their
cross daily and follow me." The cross his followers are to take up
daily is obedience to his teachings, summarized by him in two Great
Commandments: " 'You shall love the Lord your God with all your
heart, and with all your soul, and with all your mind.' This is the
greatest and first commandment. And a second is like it: 'You shall
love your neighbor as yourself." On these two commandments hang
all the law and the prophets" (Matt. 22:37-40). God gives us the
grace needed to daily take up our cross and follow Jesus.

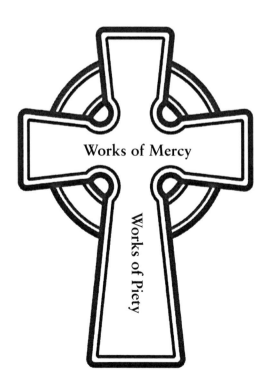

The cross provides a rich and fitting image for the life of discipleship. The vertical beam of the cross is the divine-human relationship. The works of piety (acts of worship and devotion such as prayer, the Lord's Supper, reading scripture, listening to the word read and proclaimed, and fasting) are how we love God. The works of piety are how we participate in our relationship with God. They are similar to what we do with and for a loved one. We look forward to spending time with our beloved to listen, touch, share food and drink, and take part in activities he or she enjoys. When we love someone, we want to be one with her or him. The works of piety are practices that bring us into God's presence. They help us share in God's life and open our hearts to his love.

The horizontal beam is our relationship with those whom God loves. The works of mercy (acts of compassion and justice; see Matt. 25:31-46 and Luke 10:25-37) are how Christians love those whom God loves. When we love someone, we want to spend time with their friends. Hanging out with our beloved's friends helps us more deeply understand who he or she is. When Christians serve and love the least, the last, and the lost of this world, they spend time with God's friends:

> The poor as Jesus' bosom-friends,
> The poor he makes his latest care,
> To all his followers commends,
> And wills us on our hands to bear;
> The poor our dearest care we make,
> And love them for our Savior's sake.[6]

Love is at the center of the cross, because "God is love" (1 John 4:7-21). God's love enables us to take up our cross daily. "In this is love, not that we loved God but that he loved us and sent his Son to be the atoning sacrifice for our sins" (1 John 4:10).

The goal of Methodism is to form a "people who profess to pursue (in whatsoever measure they have attained) holiness of heart and life, inward and outward conformity in all things to the revealed will of God; who place religion in an uniform resemblance of the great object of it; in a steady imitation of Him they worship, in all his imitable perfections; more particularly, in justice, mercy, and truth, or universal love filling the heart, and governing the life."[7] The General Rules are a simple, practical guide for following Jesus Christ in the world. We love those whom God loves by "doing no harm by avoiding evil" and by "doing good, by being in every way merciful." We love God with all our heart, soul, and mind "by practicing the ordinances of God: the public worship of God; the ministry of the Word, either read or expounded; the Lord's Supper; family and private prayer; searching the Scriptures; and fasting or abstinence."

When we accept Jesus' challenge to deny ourselves, take up our cross daily and follow him, we become people who know the love of God (Luke 9:23). And people who have never known or experienced God's love experience it through our practice of compassion and justice in Christ's name.

The theological term for restoration of relationship with God is *justification*. It is God's work for us through Christ crucified and risen. Justification is God's pure gift. Nothing we could ever do or say could earn this gift. Otherwise it would not be a gift. It is the work of grace for each of us, restoring us to relationship with God and giving us the gift of faith. By faith God enables us to respond to God's love and to grow in trust and love.

Holiness: The Goal of Discipleship

John Wesley frequently said a Christian is a person "with the mind of Christ who walked just as he walked." By this he meant that a Christian is a person who has experienced the inner change of heart and mind that Christ does for us by grace in justification (Phil. 2:5). This is pure gift! It is the beginning of a new way of life shaped by grace working in the believer, enabling him or her to "walk just as he walked" (1 John 2:6). This is the work of sanctifying grace, which conquers the sin that remains within and forms new ways of thinking and behaving. Wesley called these "holy tempers." The apostle Paul called them "fruit of the Spirit": love, joy, peace, patience, kindness, generosity, faithfulness, gentleness, and self-control (Gal. 5:22-23).

At the moment of justification (God's work for us in Christ crucified
and risen), the Holy Spirit begins to work in us to heal and restore
the damage sin has done. Sanctifying grace works in us, enabling
us to cooperate with the Spirit's work of restoring the soul and the
image of Christ. By grace we may "walk just as he walked."

John Wesley described how Christians cooperate with the work
of the Holy Spirit in his sermon titled "On Zeal." In this brief paragraph he uses the image of five concentric circles to describe the goal
of the Christian life and the means to attaining it:

> In a Christian believer love sits upon the throne which is erected
> in the inmost soul; namely, love of God and man, which fills
> the whole heart, and reigns without a rival. In a circle near the
> throne are all holy tempers;—longsuffering, gentleness, meek-
> ness, fidelity, temperance; and if any other were comprised in
> "the mind which was in Christ Jesus." In an exterior circle are
> all the works of mercy, whether to the souls or bodies of men.
> By these we exercise all holy tempers; by these we continu-
> ally improve them, so that all these are real means of grace,
> although this is not commonly adverted to. Next to these are
> those that are usually termed works of piety;—reading and
> hearing the word, public, family, private prayer, receiving the
> Lord's Supper, fasting or abstinence. Lastly, that his followers
> may the more effectually provoke one another to love, holy
> tempers, and good works, our blessed Lord has united them
> together in one body, the Church, dispersed all over the earth;
> a little emblem of which, of the Church universal, we have in
> every particular Christian congregation.[8]

Provoking One Another to Love: The Purpose of the Church

In the fifth circle, the church is the community that provides the
means that makes all the other practices possible. Wesley says the

purpose of the church is to "more effectually provoke one another to love, holy tempers, and good works." He is referring to Hebrews 10:23-25 (emphasis added): "Let us hold fast to the confession of our hope without wavering, for he who has promised is faithful. *And let us consider how to provoke one another to love and good deeds*, not neglecting to meet together, as is the habit of some, but encouraging one another, and all the more as you see the Day approaching." The word *provoke* is typically used with anger, wrath, fighting, and violence. But here the writer of Hebrews and Wesley use the word to help us understand that the pursuit of holiness happens in the company of others who lead by example. He is saying the purpose of Christian community is to incite one another to lives of love and good works.

We see this reflected in the words of the baptismal covenant when the congregation promises "with God's help we will proclaim the good news and live according to the example of Christ. We will surround these persons with a community of love and forgiveness, that they may grow in their trust of God, and be found faithful in their service to others. We will pray for them, that they may be true disciples who walk in the way that leads to life."[9] This is another way of saying that we are united in Christ to "provoke one another to love, holy tempers, and good works." Baptism marks the initiation into the church and provides the ongoing shape of the Christian life. When the church is serious about baptism it is organized to provoke members to love and good works.

Participation in a congregation that promises to surround us with a community of love and forgiveness and that does all in its power to increase faith, confirm hope, and perfect us in love equips us to cooperate with the Holy Spirit through formation of new habits (loving God and loving who God loves). These new habits enable the Holy Spirit to shape new ways of thinking and behaving, what Wesley called "holy tempers." Wesley called the "holy tempers": love, joy, peace, patience, kindness, generosity, faithfulness, gentleness, and self-control (Gal. 5:22-23). Life in a church that encourages and supports growth in holiness of heart and life through practicing works of piety and works of mercy leads to persons who have "the mind of Christ" and who "walk just as he walked."

Conclusion: The Power of God—Love

Love is the power of God. Jesus Christ is the incarnation of God's love for the world (John 3:16). To learn what love is and what it looks like, look to Jesus Christ's life, death, and resurrection. The most complete description of this love is provided by the apostle Paul in 1 Corinthians 13:1-13. "Love is patient; love is kind; love is not envious or boastful or arrogant or rude. It does not insist on its own way; it is not irritable or resentful; it does not rejoice in wrongdoing, but rejoices in the truth. It bears all things, believes all things, hopes all things, endures all things. Love never ends" (vv. 4-8a). Love is the power of God that brings forth life, righteousness, and justice. Love overcomes the powers of sin and death that naturally reign in the human heart. When Christians cooperate with and participate in the redeeming and healing work of the Holy Spirit, we are set free from sin's power to diminish and destroy life. Grace, which is God's love at work in our hearts and in the world, sets us free to become the persons God created us to be, in the image of Christ.

Love ruling in the believer's heart is the outcome of the Christian life. The Wesleyan way of making disciples of Jesus Christ is directed toward teaching and equipping people to pursue holiness of heart and life, which is another way of saying love ruling the heart and governing the life of the Christian. Love is the beginning and the end of the Christian life.

Now by this we may be sure that we know him, if we obey his commandments. Whoever says, "I have come to know him," but does not obey his commandments, is a liar, and in such a person the truth does not exist; but whoever obeys his word, truly in this person the love of God has reached perfection. By this we may be sure that we are in him: whoever says, "I abide in him," ought to walk just as he walked. (1 John 2:3-6)

This passage echoes the words of Jesus from Matthew 7 that began this chapter. The writer makes the connection between obedience to Jesus and the holiness that follows. Following and obeying Jesus will change the hearts and lives of people who receive the waters of baptism and take up the Christian life. Wesley famously wrote that there are no solitary Christians. By this he meant that following Jesus in the world necessarily requires participation in a community devoted to him, in the company of others who know him and who are pursuing "the mind of Christ" so they may "walk just as he walked."

The Christian life is a relational endeavor. Christians need relationships with women and men who have experience walking with Jesus in the world. Covenant Discipleship groups serve as the solid foundation of discipleship the congregation needs to carry out its mission of making disciples of Jesus Christ for the transformation of the world.

> As colleagues of the risen Christ, helping to fulfill God's plan of salvation, Christian disciples have a clear identity. They are heralds of *shalom*. They are salt, light, leaven, and seed of the coming reign of God (Matt. 5:13-14; 13:31-33). To accept this identity means a very intentional way of life; which is why "disciple" and "discipline" come from the same Latin word, *discipulus*. This is best translated today as a "special student," someone who has undertaken to study with a particular teacher in great depth, and who therefore has arranged his or her life to make such study possible. Christian disciples must expect to order their priorities in the same way, and arrange their lives so that they are "disciplines" in following the teachings of Jesus.
>
> —David Lowes Watson
> *Forming Christian Disciples*, p. 6

CHAPTER 2

Living as Witnesses: The General Rule of Discipleship

To witness to Jesus Christ in the world
and to follow his teachings through acts of
compassion, justice, worship, and devotion
under the guidance of the Holy Spirit.

*—The Book of Discipline of
The United Methodist Church 2012,* ¶1117.2

The ancient Christian practice of a rule of life, as described in the introduction, is a set of agreed-upon spiritual disciplines aimed at helping members grow together in holiness of heart and life; loving God with all their heart, soul, and mind; and loving those whom God loves, as God loves them. The rule of life for The United Methodist Church is its General Rules. The General Rule of Discipleship, quoted above, is a contemporary adaptation of the General Rules for use in United Methodist congregations. I recommend congregations adopt the General Rule of Discipleship as their rule of life, to shape their missional life.

Social Holiness

The Christian life is shaped by obedience to Jesus' teachings. The General Rule of Discipleship shapes the life and work of Covenant Discipleship groups, class leaders, and the congregation. It helps them live as witnesses to Jesus Christ in the world as they follow his teachings.

In the baptismal covenant we promise to "confess Jesus Christ as your Savior, put your whole trust in his grace, and promise to serve him as your Lord, in union with the church." The congregation, in turn, promises to proclaim the good news and live according to the example of Christ; to surround the baptized with a community of love and forgiveness, that we may grow in our trust of God and be found faithful in our service to others; to pray for us, that we may be true disciples who walk in the way that leads to life.[1] Living the baptismal covenant is how Christians obey Jesus' "new commandment": "I give you a new commandment, that you love one another. Just as I have loved you, you also should love one another. By this everyone will know that you are my disciples, if you have love for one another" (John 13:34-35). When Christians "watch over one another in love" and help each other grow in holiness of heart and life, they keep this new commandment. Congregations keep Jesus' new commandment when they intentionally develop a path to discipleship that meets people where they are and provides guides along the way in the form of small groups and seasoned disciples.

This is what John Wesley meant when he wrote: "Solitary religion is not to be found there. 'Holy Solitaries' is a phrase no more consistent with the gospel than Holy Adulterers. The gospel of Christ knows of no religion, but social; no holiness but social holiness. Faith working by love, is the length and breadth and depth and height of Christian perfection."[2] Wesley believed living the Christian life requires community centered in the life and mission of Jesus Christ. Christians are responsible for one another. In Sermon 92, "On Zeal," he described the purpose the church formed by Christ in order for the members to "more effectually provoke one another to love, holy tempers, and good works." The General Rule of Discipleship is a handy guide for "provoking one another to love and good works" (Heb. 10:25).

When Wesley says that holiness is social, he means that the depth of our love for God is revealed by the way we love those whom God loves. If we truly love God, then we must love our brother and sister in Christ and our neighbor (1 John 4:19-21). This requires us to be in relationships with the people God places alongside us in the church and the people of our neighborhood, our city, and the world. We need community, what Wesley calls "society," for grace to nurture us into the persons God created us to be. The baptismal covenant describes the relationship between God, the baptized, and the church. The General Rule of Discipleship provides the means for living the covenant and becoming agents of social holiness.

"To Witness to Jesus Christ in the World"

In its opening words, the General Rule of Discipleship emphasizes *witness* as characterizing the Christian life. A witness has personal knowledge and experience of a person, place, thing, or event and is prepared to give evidence. Christians are witnesses to Jesus Christ because they know him, experience his love, and testify to what he is up to in the world. They give evidence of Jesus' love and power when they renounce wickedness, reject evil, and repent of their sin. Christians witness to Jesus Christ when they accept the freedom and power he gives to resist evil, injustice, and oppression. Their lives give testimony to him when they confess Jesus Christ as Lord and join his work of preparing this world for the coming reign of God.

Witnesses are sometimes welcomed. Their testimony is received as good news that brings joy and liberation. They are celebrated and honored as truth tellers. Other times witnesses are received with indifference. Their testimony is ignored. They are seen as curiosities or light entertainment, but not received and taken seriously. Sometimes the gospel of God's coming reign is not welcome. It offends and threatens the status que, bringing violence and persecution upon the witness.

Jesus and his apostles experienced all these responses, as have witnesses to Jesus Christ throughout history. Some were received with joy. Others were ignored like Paul in Athens (Acts 17:16-34). You are probably familiar with the Latin word *martyr*, which means "witness." Today, the word *martyr* means a person who suffers for their beliefs. Martyrs sometimes suffer to the point of death. We know from the history of Christianity that countless Christian women and men have suffered and died because of their loyalty to Jesus Christ and his good news of God's coming reign on earth as in heaven. Their lives, and deaths, tell us that being a witness to Jesus Christ in the world is often dangerous business.

Jesus knew his disciples would face fear and opposition. That is why he appeared to them after his crucifixion on the day of his resurrection saying, "Peace be with you. As the Father has sent me, so I send you." . . . He breathed on them and said, "Receive the Holy Spirit" (John 20:21-22). In this encounter with the risen Christ, the disciples are commissioned to go into the world as witnesses to him and his good news for the world. He equips them with his peace, which is his presence with them. He also gives them the Holy Spirit to inspire and guide them along the way. In another encounter, the risen Christ commissioned his disciples, saying, "Go therefore and make disciples of all nations, baptizing them in the name of the Father and of the Son and of the Holy Spirit, and teaching them to obey everything that I have commanded you. And remember, I am with you always, to the end of the age" (Matt. 28:19-20). He promises to be with his disciples as they walk and live as witnesses to him and his good news for the world.

John Wesley knew very well the blessings and challenges of living as a witness to Jesus Christ in the world. On April 2, 1739, the day he first preached outdoors in England he wrote in his journal:

> At four in the afternoon, I submitted to be more vile and proclaimed in the highways the glad tidings of salvation, speaking from a little eminence in a ground adjoining to the city, to about three thousand people. The Scripture on which I

spoke was this (is it possible anyone should be ignorant that it is fulfilled in every true minister of Christ?): "The Spirit of the Lord is upon me, because he hath anointed me to preach the gospel to the poor; he hath sent me to heal the broken-hearted, to preach deliverance to the captives, and recovering of sight to the blind, to set at liberty them that are bruised, to proclaim the acceptable year of the Lord" (Luke 4:18-19).[3]

His preaching was received as good news by some while many listened with indifferent curiosity. On the other hand, it was not uncommon for his audience to throw stones and garbage at Wesley and other Methodist preachers while they witnessed to Christ and salvation by grace through faith.

Witnessing to Jesus Christ in the world requires baptism by water and the Spirit. It is possible only when we are part of the community centered in the life and work of Jesus, equipped and empowered by his Holy Spirit. To live as his witnesses in the world requires us to participate in a congregation devoted to doing all in its power to increase our faith, to confirm our hope in Christ, and to perfect us in love. The congregation must do all in its power to help its members live the baptismal covenant.[4]

Witnesses to Jesus Christ in the world are formed, equipped, and supported best in small groups with other witnesses. The early Methodist class meetings are excellent examples of such groups.[5] Blockages to grace are removed when Christians meet weekly to "watch over one another in love," to pray for one another, to sing hymns of praise to our Lord, to give an account of what we have done to witness to Jesus Christ in the world. As trust grows among us, our faith in Christ increases. As we grow closer to one another, we grow closer to Christ.

"And to Follow His Teachings"

Christians live as witnesses to Jesus Christ in the world by following and obeying his teachings. Of course, the primary source we have for Jesus' teaching is the four Gospels found in the New Testament. John

Wesley believed Jesus' teachings are conveyed most succinctly in the Sermon on the Mount (Matt. 5:1—7:28). He published a collection of thirteen sermons on the Sermon on the Mount. The teachings contained in these three chapters capture Jesus' teaching on the coming reign of God and the promises and the expectations of life as citizens of God's kingdom. Wesley's sermons give helpful, practical guidance for the Christian life in a world opposed to God's righteousness and justice.

Jesus' teachings in the Sermon on the Mount tell us the kingdom of God is very different from the world we know and experience every day. The kingdom of God turns the world as we know it upside down. This is evident from the beginning of the sermon when Jesus says, "Blessed are the poor in spirit, for theirs is the kingdom of heaven. Blessed are those who mourn, for they will be comforted. Blessed are the meek, for they will inherit the earth" (Matt. 5:3-5). The Beatitudes signal that the values, promises, and expectations of God's reign are very different from the world. Those whom the world regards as the lowly and powerless are the ones whom God blesses and honors. In God's kingdom, grace overcomes domination and violence. Love is God's power at work in the world. Love is greater than fear. Love sets people free for lives of love of God and for those whom God loves.

While the Sermon on the Mount is an excellent source for Jesus' teachings, Wesley needed a succinct summary that could be easily memorized and serve as a guide for living the life Jesus describes. He believed Jesus summarized his teachings in the saying known as the Great Commandment, found in Matthew 22:34-40:

> When the Pharisees heard that he had silenced the Sadducees, they gathered together, and one of them, a lawyer, asked him a question to test him. "Teacher, which commandment in the law is the greatest?" He said to him, " 'You shall love the Lord your God with all your heart, and with all your soul, and with all your mind.' This is the greatest and first commandment. And a second is like it: 'You shall love your neighbor as yourself.' On these two commandments hang all the law and the prophets."

These commandments serve as the guiding principle for living the Christian life. He repeatedly cites them as being the guide and goal (*telos*) of Christian discipleship. They describe both the process and the outcome of holiness of heart and life.

Holiness of heart is the inward change in attitudes, thinking, and habits. They are reformed by grace through the work of the Holy Spirit when we first accept God's love, and then participate in that love through the disciplines of worship, sacrament, scripture, and prayer. These spiritual disciplines are gifts from God, used by people for millennia, as ways to participate in the relationship God initiates in baptism. God brings us into the community of the church to provide the teaching, support, and accountability we need to love God with all our heart, soul, and mind. In the church we experience God's love through relationships with people striving to love God alongside us.

Holiness of life is loving our neighbor as ourselves. If we truly love God with all our heart, soul, and mind, if we strive for holiness of heart, then we must love those whom God loves, as God loves them. Jesus teaches his followers that our neighbors are more than the people who live around us, who look, behave, and think like us. Jesus expands the neighbor to include anyone anywhere in the world who needs love and mercy (see Matt. 5:3-12; 25:31-46). He broadens the identity of neighbor even more in Matthew 5:43-48 when Jesus tells his followers:

> You have heard that it was said, "You shall love your neighbor and hate your enemy." But I say to you, Love your enemies and pray for those who persecute you, so that you may be children of your Father in heaven; for he makes his sun rise on the evil and on the good, and sends rain on the righteous and on the unrighteous. For if you love those who love you, what reward do you have? Do not even the tax collectors do the same? And if you greet only your brothers and sisters, what more are you doing than others? Do not even the Gentiles do the same? Be perfect, therefore, as your heavenly Father is perfect.

Jesus tells his followers we are to imitate him. If we follow him, he will teach and equip us to love as God loves, which means loving even our enemies. Such love is humanly impossible. But with Christ, in the midst of Christian community, even such love becomes possible (Matt. 19:26; Luke 1:37). The apostle Paul writes, "I can do all things through him who strengthens me" (Phil. 4:13). That line appears at the conclusion of a litany of Paul's experience of love and support in Christian community.

Holiness of life is possible when we cooperate with grace among the people and relationships God provides in the community of the baptized. Christ walks in and alongside us as we participate in the baptismal covenant. Living in the midst of a community that promises to surround us with prayer, love, and forgiveness, we become "perfect . . . as your heavenly Father is perfect." In his letter to the Ephesians, Paul puts it this way: "We must grow up in every way into him who is the head, into Christ, from whom the whole body, joined and knit together by every ligament with which it is equipped, as each part is working properly, promotes the body's growth in building itself up in love" (Eph. 4:15-16).

Charles Wesley succinctly describes the process and goal of discipleship and salvation in the following stanzas:

> Plead we thus for faith alone,
> Faith which by our works is shown;
> God it is who justifies,
> Only faith the grace applies,
> Active faith that lives within,
> Conquers earth, and hell, and sin,
> Sanctifies, and makes us whole,
> Forms the Savior in the soul.
>
> Let us for this faith contend,
> Sure salvation is its end;
> Heaven already is begun,
> Everlasting life is won.

Only let us persevere
Till we see our Lord appear;
Never from the rock remove,
Saved by faith which works by love.[6]

For the Wesley brothers, "active faith that lives within" is balanced between loving God with all our heart, soul, and mind and loving those whom God loves; holiness of heart and life. The two are intimately connected and keep Christians centered in Christ, rather than in ourselves or our personal temperament. The discipline of loving God through acts of worship and devotion is how we participate in a relationship with God. Our relationship with God opens our hearts, minds, and hands to the world and the world's people. The grace God pours into our hearts gives us eyes to see and ears to hear the cries of the world's people who are hungry, sick, homeless, and in prison. More than hearing their cries, through grace we are equipped and sent to them in acts of compassion and justice. Participating with God in acts of compassion, justice, worship, and devotion is how Christians grow in holiness and how God's love "forms the Savior in the soul."

Balance

The General Rule of Discipleship helps Christians to be mindful that Jesus calls his followers to obey all his teachings, and not only those we are temperamentally inclined to practice. He knew that some are drawn to the first commandment: "You shall love the Lord your God with all your heart, and with all your soul, and with all your mind" (Matt. 22:37). They are drawn to fervent worship, prayer, and other works of piety. Some of these people are introverts who are attracted to the inward life with God, while an extrovert may be drawn to outward acts of worship and justice. For example, as an introvert, I am more comfortable with devotional practices of personal prayer, reflection, study, and writing. I need the support and accountability provided by my Covenant Discipleship group to help me be more balanced in my discipleship. Our covenant and weekly meetings help me to be conscious of my need to look for opportunities God gives each week to be a channel of grace in the world through acts of compassion and justice.

When I was a pastor in Duluth, Minnesota, I started a Covenant Discipleship group with members of the congregation. Our covenant included a clause that said we would give four hours of service with poor and homeless people each month. After several weeks of listening to me tell how I did not fulfill this clause of our covenant, one group member informed me that I could expect a telephone call from the executive director of Churches United in Ministry (CHUM) inviting me to serve on the board. The group had heard that CHUM was looking for a clergyperson to serve on its board. They recognized that I needed help with our covenant clause to be in service among poor and homeless people and nominated me for the board position. My group strongly encouraged me to accept the invitation. When the call came, I said yes.

At my first meeting of the CHUM board, I was assigned to be responsible for the Drop-in Center. Located in the heart of Duluth, "The Drop" serves as a living room for the poor. It is a safe place for people to spend the day, store their belongings, receive mail, do laundry, and bathe. Social workers are available to help guests navigate the social service systems of St. Louis County and the state of Minnesota. I made several visits to The Drop to meet staff and guests. During those visits I found much good work that was meeting the physical and material needs of the people. The only thing missing, given that it was run by a Christian organization, was pastoral ministry with the people. In conversation with guests, I learned they needed someone to listen to them, to pray with them, visit them in the hospital and jail.

When I brought my report to the board, I also brought a recommendation to develop a weekly pastoral presence at The Drop. The board's response was positive. They unanimously recommended that I develop the weekly pastoral ministry.

This led to me working with the Drop-in Center director to lead a Bible study every Friday morning. For the next four years he and I led a lectionary Bible study with Drop-in Center guests. I told the people of the congregation I served that if they needed me on Friday mornings they could find me at the CHUM Drop-in Center. Depending upon the week, we had six to twenty people show up for Bible study. We read and discussed the Gospel lesson for the week. In addition to the conversation centered on the Gospel, we sang favorite hymns and praise songs. I found that many of the homeless women and men knew their Bible and had plenty to say. We always closed our time with identifying prayer concerns and then sharing a rich time of prayer.

The weekly Bible study led to relationships and building trust with the people. Most weeks one or more persons would ask me to stay to pray with them. I was asked to preside at an annual memorial service for guests who died during the year. I soon found myself looking forward to Friday mornings and to what God had in store for us each week.

I'm telling this story to illustrate how the balanced discipleship presented in the General Rule of Discipleship and reflected in the group covenant produces growth in holiness of heart and life. My experience at the Drop-in Center taught me that when I get outside of my comfort zone I am more vulnerable to the power of grace to form me into the person God created me to be. I received much more from the people at the Drop-in Center than I ever gave to them. They taught me more about the nature of discipleship, the grace in their lives, and friendship than I could ever learn from a book. I will always be thankful to the people of that Covenant Discipleship group in Duluth for lovingly pushing me out the door of the church. They helped this introvert grow in holiness of heart and life.

The General Rule of Discipleship helps both the introvert and the extrovert be more mindful of their need for balance. We are encouraged to get out of our comfort zones to go to people and places we are likely to avoid if left to our own preferences.

The Faith of a Servant or a Child?

Other people focus on the first commandment of Jesus because they ascribe to an overloaded doctrine of justification. By this I mean they rightly believe we are saved by grace through faith. "For by grace you have been saved through faith, and this is not your own doing; it is the gift of God—not the results of works, so that no one may boast" (Eph. 2:8-9). We are saved from the powers of sin and death by Christ crucified and risen. It is entirely God's work of love for us on the hard wood of the cross. Nothing we could ever do or say could make us deserving of this amazing grace. All we need to do to receive the gift is to accept God's love in Jesus Christ and believe the good news.

This is all true. It is what scripture teaches and what John Wesley preached and taught. However, this overloaded doctrine of justification is not the whole story. I describe it as "overloaded" because the problem, as I see it, is that faith is reduced to simple belief or agreement with a creed or statement such as "Jesus Christ is my personal Savior." And believing is all that is required. The emphasis is upon holiness of heart; getting our heart right with God through faith in Jesus Christ. Holiness of life, loving our neighbor as ourselves, is optional, because good works are not required. Some believe good works could lead to pride and believing that we can earn God's love. They believe it is better to trust in the promise that we are saved by grace through faith in God's Son, crucified and risen. He paid the price of our salvation. All we need to do is believe in him.

John Wesley called this the faith of a servant. Those who believe, expect to receive eternal life in return for believing. Faith is seen as an exchange between the believer and God. The believer believes, and God responds by accepting the believer into God's favor and as a citizen of God's kingdom. Servants do what is required of them. When they fulfill their duty, servants receive the wages due them.

The faith of a servant emphasizes the gospel about Jesus (see Acts 10:34-43). It is the good news that we are saved by grace through faith. Eternal life in God's kingdom is given to all who believe that

Jesus Christ is God's Son and that he suffered and died on the cross to take away our sins. Our sins are forgiven. He took all the sins of the world into himself and paid the price so we don't have to.

Wesley believed that scripture teaches there is more to the story and to God's grace. He believed that God created us to be more than servants. We are created to be and to live as God's children. The faith of a servant is the beginning of the way of salvation. The goal is the faith of a child. As we participate in the baptized community of the church and small groups that provide accountability and support for growth in holiness of heart and life, as we cooperate with the grace given and the work of the Holy Spirit, we will grow into the faith of a child. We will receive the "spirit of adoption": "For you did not receive a spirit of slavery to fall back into fear, but you have received a spirit of adoption. When we cry, 'Abba! Father!' it is that very Spirit bearing witness with our spirit that we are children of God, and if children, then heirs, heirs of God and joint heirs with Christ—if, in fact, we suffer with him so that we may also be glorified with him" (Rom. 8:15-17).

The faith of a child of God obeys Christ out of love. The child imitates the parent, with the desire to take on the character of the parent. This is why Jesus says to his disciples, "If you love me, you will keep my commandments" (John 14:15). Love motivates the child to obey and to imitate the parent, because the child wants to be like his or her beloved.

The faith of a child believes and obeys the gospel about Jesus *and* the gospel of Jesus. This is what the apostle Paul meant when he wrote, "For by grace you have been saved through faith, and this is not your own doing; it is the gift of God—not the result of works, so that no one may boast. *For we are what he has made us, created in Christ Jesus for good works, which God prepared beforehand to be our way of life*" (Eph. 2:8-10, emphasis added). The gospel proclaimed by Jesus is found in Mark 1:15: "The time is fulfilled, and the kingdom of God has come near; repent, and believe the good news." Everywhere he traveled, Jesus preached and taught the good news of God's reign on earth as it is in heaven. He summarizes life in God's reign when he read from the book of the prophet Isaiah in the Nazareth synagogue:

> The Spirit of the Lord is upon me,
>   because he has anointed me
>   to bring good news to the poor.
> He has sent me to proclaim release to the captives
>   and recovery of sight to the blind,
>   to let the oppressed go free,
> to proclaim the year of the Lord's favor. (Luke 4:18-19)

Jesus summarized the Christian life for children of God and citizens of God's reign: "If any want to become my followers, let them deny themselves and take up their cross daily and follow me" (Luke 9:23).

This is how we grow from the faith of a servant into the faith of a child. As we participate in the relationship with Christ, the Holy Spirit works in us, by grace, to experience God's love. When we love God, that love equips us to love those whom God loves. Grace equips us to live the Jesus way (Luke 9:23).

Self-denial is the essence of love. It is the self-emptying Paul describes in Philippians 2:5-8 (emphasis added):

> Let the same mind be in you that was in Christ Jesus,
>   who, though he was in the form of God,
>   did not regard equality with God
>   as something to be exploited,
>   *but emptied himself,*
>   taking the form of a slave,
>   being born in human likeness.
> And being found in human form
>   he humbled himself
>   and became obedient to the point of death—
>   even death on a cross.

This way of love equips us to put others first and self second. Our eyes, ears, heart, and hands are open to the world God loves. We notice people the world ignores. We serve and love people the world hates. The faith of a child seeks to be good news to the poor.

The cross Jesus calls his followers to take up is obedience to his teachings (Matt. 7:24-29; Luke 6:46-49; John 14:15; 15:14). He summarized his teachings in the two commandments to love God with all our heart, soul, and mind and to love our neighbor as ourselves (Matt. 22:37-39). The vertical beam of the cross represents our relationship with God. The horizontal beam of the cross represents our relationship with our neighbor. The neighbor is anyone anywhere in the world who is in need of compassion and justice.

The balanced, cross-bearing discipleship Jesus calls his followers to is represented by the image of the Jerusalem Cross:

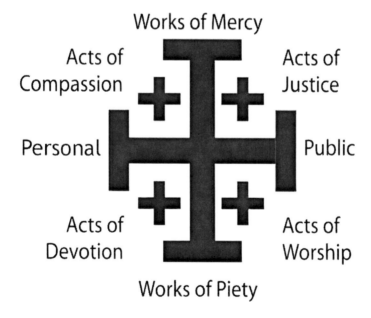

The Means of Grace

In his sermon titled "The Means of Grace," Wesley wrote, "By 'means of grace' I understand outward signs, words, or actions ordained of God, and appointed for this end—to be the *ordinary* channels whereby he might convey to *people* preventing, justifying, or sanctifying grace" (emphasis added).[7] The means of grace are practices God gives, and Jesus teaches, to open our hearts to God's love for us and for the world. The way of salvation requires our participation. Wesley quoted St. Augustine to illustrate the responsible nature of grace and salvation: " 'He that made us without ourselves, will not save us without ourselves.' [God] will not save us unless we 'save ourselves from this untoward generation' (Acts 2:40), unless we ourselves 'fight the good fight of faith, and lay hold on eternal life' (1 Tim. 6:12), unless we 'agonize to enter in at the strait gate' (Luke 13:24), 'deny ourselves, and take up our cross daily' (Luke 9:23), and labor, by every possible means to 'make our own calling and election sure' (2 Pet. 1:10)."[8]

Works of Piety—Loving God

Works of piety are the means of grace that open our heart to God. Wesley identified six essential works of piety in the third General Rule:

- The public worship of God
- The ministry of the Word, either read or expounded
- The Supper of the Lord
- Family and private prayer
- Searching the scriptures
- Fasting or abstinence

The first three works in this list are *acts of worship.* These are practices Christians do together when they gather to offer themselves in service to God. They build one another up in love through communal praise, confession, prayer, proclamation, singing, and sacrament. The second half of the list are the *acts of devotion.* They are practices we do alone with God to open ourselves to grace each day, to nurture our personal relationship with the one who loves us beyond measure.

Acts of Devotion

Acts of devotion are the *personal* works of piety. They are means of grace we practice alone with God. John Wesley lists three essential acts of devotion in the third General Rule ("by attending upon all the ordinances of God"):

- Personal and family prayer
- Searching the scriptures
- Fasting or abstinence

Prayer and searching the scriptures are daily practices that often accompany one another. Reading and meditating on the scriptures often leads to time in prayer. Lectio Divina is an ancient practice in which reading scripture leads the Christian into prayer. Reading and meditating upon devotional classics or a resource like *A Disciple's Journal* or *The Upper Room* helps to center the day on Christ.

Several years ago I saw the movie *Shadowlands* in which Anthony Hopkins plays the British writer and theologian C. S. Lewis. The film tells the story of Lewis and his relationship with his wife, Joy Gresham, played by Debra Winger. While Joy was in the hospital being treated for cancer, Lewis spent days and nights at her bedside. One day they received the good news that Joy's cancer was in remission. Lewis then returned to his teaching duties at Magdalen College. As he was putting on his teaching gown, several of his friends came to Lewis to express their joy and relief at the good news. They also acknowledged Lewis's persistence in prayer at Joy's bedside. Lewis's response has always stuck with me. It is a useful reminder about the nature, purpose, and importance of prayer: "I pray because I can't help myself. I pray because I'm helpless. I pray because the need flows out of me all the time—waking and sleeping. It doesn't change God—it changes me."

Wesley wrote, "God does nothing but in answer to prayer. . . . On every occasion of uneasiness we should retire to prayer, that we may give place to the grace and light of God, and then form our resolutions, without being in any pain about what success they may have."[9]

Prayer is like breathing to the Christian. It is necessary for life in God to grow and bear fruit in us and for God's kingdom:

> All who desire the grace of God are to wait for it in the way of prayer. This is the express direction of our Lord himself. In his Sermon upon the Mount, after explaining at large wherein religion consists, and describing the main branches of it, he adds, "Ask, and it shall be given you; seek, and ye shall find; knock, and it shall be opened unto you: For everyone that asketh receiveth; and he that seeketh findeth; and to him that knocketh it shall be opened." (Matt. 7:7, 8) Here we are in the plainest manner directed to ask, in order to, or as a means of, receiving; to seek, in order to find, the grace of God, the pearl of great price; and to knock, to continue asking and seeking, if we would enter into his kingdom.[10]

Searching the scriptures is another essential means of grace.[11] Wesley, of course, refers to scripture to make his point that searching the scripture is an essential practice for the Christian life. He cites John 5:39: "[Jesus said] You search the scriptures because you think that in them you have eternal life; and it is they that testify on my behalf." Wesley believed the scriptures contained all that was necessary for salvation and living the Christian life. The books of the Old and New Testament are God's gift to the world to reveal the way of life that leads to holiness of heart and life.

Wesley refers us to 2 Timothy 3:16-17: "All scripture is inspired by God and is useful for teaching, for reproof, for correction, and for training in righteousness, so that everyone who belongs to God may be proficient, equipped for every good work." He makes the point that the "scripture" Paul refers to here is the books of the Old Testament, as the New Testament had not yet been written. Wesley's point here is that all scripture is essential for Christian teaching and formation. Wesley encourages Methodists to read, study, meditate, and pray with the word of God contained in the scriptures of the Old and

New Testament. In the Book we encounter the living Lord who leads us to righteousness and equips us to join him in "every good work."

Fasting is another ancient means of grace. Wesley practiced fasting at least one day a week for most of his life. He believed it to be an essential practice, because Jesus fasted and taught his disciples to do the same (Matt. 6:16-18). And fasting leads to prayer. It is a simple way Christians can imitate Christ who "emptied himself" (Phil. 2:7) and become one with humankind as a humble servant. Charles Wesley describes Jesus' self-emptying love in the third stanza of his great hymn, "And Can It Be That I Should Gain" (emphasis added):

> He left his Father's throne above,
> So free, so infinite his grace;
> *Emptied himself of all but love,*
> And bled for Adam's helpless race;
> 'Tis mercy all, immense and free;
> For, O my God, it found out me.

When we fast we empty ourselves and become more aware of our dependence upon God's good gifts of food and drink that sustain our life. Fasting also places us in solidarity with the people of the earth for whom fasting is not a choice. Christ suffers for them every day. Wesley encouraged Methodists to pray for and give alms to the poor when they fast.

Acts of devotion keep the heart open to grace that keeps us centered in Christ and what he is up to in our life and in the world. When the heart is open to grace, it becomes more and more open to the world that God loves, which means that acts of devotion equip us for and lead us to acts of compassion and justice.

Acts of Worship

Acts of worship are the *social and public* works of piety. They are what Christians do together when they gather in Christ's name (Matt. 18:20). Through praise, confession, reading scripture, proclamation, prayer, offering gifts, confession, thanksgiving, receiving the sacrament, and sending the gathered into the world again, the Christian community builds one another up in love and offers itself in service to God and the world that God loves. In worship the church lifts the world and itself to God in prayer. In worship Christians experience God's presence and power. We gather to confess our sins, to receive assurance that we are forgiven, and to eat and drink Christ's body and blood, and we are sent into the world to serve as Christ's witnesses.

John Wesley lists three acts of worship in the third General Rule:

- The public worship of God
- The ministry of the Word, whether read or expounded
- The Lord's Supper

Methodists were expected to participate in worship on Sunday morning in their parish church and at other times throughout the week. Wesley wanted the Methodist people to be salt and light for the church. By this he meant being faithful in the worship of God through praise, prayer, proclamation, sacrament, and service.

The "ministry of the Word" is listening to the Word of God as it is read aloud. It also includes listening to preaching and interpretation of scripture by preachers and other seasoned Christians.

In addition to being an evangelical renewal movement for the church, the Methodist movement was also a eucharistic renewal movement. Charles Wesley wrote and published a collection of 166 hymns on the Lord's Supper. The Wesley brothers believed the sacrament is an essential Christian practice and means of converting and sanctifying grace. The Methodists were encouraged to participate in the sacrament as often as possible, at least once a week.

Wesley preached that participation in the Lord's Supper is Christ's command: "For I received from the Lord what I also handed on to you, that the Lord Jesus on the night when he was betrayed took a loaf of bread, and when he had given thanks, he broke it and said, 'This is my body that is for you. Do this in remembrance of me.' In the same way he took the cup also, after supper, saying, 'This cup is the new covenant in my blood. Do this, as often as you drink it, in remembrance of me.' For as often as you eat this bread and drink the cup, you proclaim the Lord's death until he comes" (1 Cor. 11:23-26).

Jesus instructed his disciples to participate in his body and blood, re-presented in the bread and wine, as often as they gather in his name until he returns. When Christians partake of the bread and cup of the Lord's Supper, we take the body and blood of Christ into ourselves. We eat and drink grace, which is medicine for our souls and bodies broken by sin and fear. At the Lord's Table, Christians receive grace that forgives our sin, restores relationship with Christ and our neighbor, and sets us free to join his mission in the world. Wesley summarizes:

> And that this is also an ordinary, stated means of receiving the grace of God, is evident from those words of the Apostle, which occur in the preceding chapter: "The cup of blessing which we bless, is it not the communion," or communication, "of the blood of Christ. The bread which we break, is it not the communion of the body of Christ" (1 Cor. 10:16). Is not the eating of that bread, and the drinking of that cup, the outward, visible means, whereby God conveys into our souls all that spiritual grace, that righteousness, and peace, and joy in the Holy Ghost, which were purchased by the body of Christ once broken and the blood of Christ once shed for us. Let all, therefore, who truly desire the grace of God, eat of that bread, and drink of that cup.[12]

Works of Mercy—Loving Those Whom God Loves

If we say we love God with all our heart, soul, and mind and profess Jesus Christ to be our Savior and Lord, then we must also strive to love those whom God loves—our neighbor and ourselves. Jesus teaches us who the neighbor is in Matthew 25:31-46. In this famous parable of the judgment of the nations, Jesus helps his followers understand their neighbor is anyone who is hungry, thirsty, a stranger, vulnerable, sick, or a prisoner. In other words, our neighbor is anyone anywhere in the world who is poor, defenseless, or oppressed. Jesus tells his followers they are duty bound to help their neighbors. Such acts of compassion and justice Wesley calls "works of mercy."

Means of Grace

John Wesley believed works of mercy are as much means of grace as works of piety: "Thus should he show his zeal for works of piety; but much more for works of mercy; seeing 'God will have mercy and not sacrifice'; that is, rather than sacrifice. Whenever, therefore, one interferes with the other, works of mercy are to be preferred. Even reading, hearing, prayer, are to be omitted, or to be postponed, 'at charity's almighty call'; when we are called to relieve the distress of our neighbor, whether in body or soul."[13] He encouraged Methodists to be mindful of opportunities every day to extend God's love into the world through simple acts of kindness to people in their neighborhood and beyond. He also says that when we are confronted with a choice between serving a suffering person right in front of us or going to a prayer meeting or worship service, then we are to always choose mercy over piety. We can always pray or go to another worship service, but the suffering of a fellow human being is immediate and must be addressed in the moment.

Works of mercy are means of grace, because when we respond to the need of a hungry, thirsty, marginalized, vulnerable, sick, or imprisoned person, we serve Christ himself. When we give food, clothing, or medicine to our neighbor who is suffering, we are doing it with, and to, Christ. Jesus says as much in Matthew 25:40: "Truly I tell you, just as you did it to one of the least of these who are members of my family, you did it to me." The people who Jesus tells us are our neighbors are also members of his family. When we serve members of his family, we serve Christ himself. This is why works of mercy are such powerful means of grace. They put us into the physical presence of our Lord and Savior. When we go to the poor, we go to meet Jesus face to face. When we meet him face to face, his love moves in our heart, soul, and mind. Wesley believed going to the poor was like medicine for the Christian, because Christ's grace has the power to heal and restore the sin-damaged image of God. This is why he says, "By [works of mercy] we exercise all holy tempers; by these we continually improve them, so that all these are real means of grace, although this is not commonly adverted to."[14]

When Christians habitually practice works of mercy, we open ourselves to the power of grace to form holy tempers in us. We allow the Holy Spirit and sanctifying grace to heal and repair our sin-damaged character, changing it into a reflection of Christ. The holy tempers are habits of the heart: love, joy, peace, patience, kindness, generosity, faithfulness, gentleness, and self-control (Gal. 5:22-23). Habitual works of mercy, empowered by works of piety, form these heart habits in the Christian. The holy tempers are like muscles that need exercise. The more we exercise them, the stronger they become. Practice also develops muscle memory, which enables us to automatically and habitually respond in love to our neighbor and the world God loves. Love becomes our natural response to the world.

> We know love by this, that he laid down his life for us—and we ought to lay down our lives for one another. How does God's love abide in anyone who has the world's goods and sees a brother or sister in need and yet refuses help? Little children, let us love, not in word or speech, but in truth and action. (1 John 3:16-18)

> There is no fear in love, but perfect love casts out fear; for fear has to do with punishment, and whoever fears has not reached perfection in love. We love because he first loved us. Those who say, "I love God," and hate their brothers or sisters, are liars; for those who do not love a brother or sister whom they have seen, cannot love God whom they have not seen. The commandment we have from him is this: those who love God must love their brothers and sisters also. (1 John 4:18-21)

Acts of Compassion

Compassion is the *personal practice* of the works of mercy. An act of compassion is a simple act of kindness to our neighbor who is hungry, thirsty, lonely, vulnerable, sick, or a prisoner. When someone tells us he is hungry, we ask him what he wants and share a meal with him or give him something to eat. When someone is mourning the death of a loved one, we go to her to pray with her, acknowledge her suffering, and share her grief. Acts of compassion are personal ways Christians habitually strive to do no harm by avoiding evil and to do good for persons who are in need, tending to both their bodies and their souls.

Wesley adds personal evangelism to the works of mercy. He believed sharing Christ and his good news of God's coming reign is one of the most important acts of compassion we can practice. When we tell a friend or acquaintance about Jesus and his reign of love and justice, we let that person know she is loved by God, who made, accepts, and yearns to draw her closer.

Acts of Justice

Acts of justice are the *social and public* works of mercy. Acts of compassion frequently lead to acts of justice. If we encounter hungry people on the streets of our town, following Jesus leads us to ask why people are hungry. What can the Christian community do to address the causes of hunger? How can the Christian community join other faith traditions and community institutions to address the causes of hunger?

Followers of Jesus are called in their baptism to accept "the freedom and power God gives to resist evil, oppression, and injustice in whatever forms they present themselves."[15] This means that professing Christians are to share in the prophetic ministry of Jesus Christ, who came to bring good news to the poor, release to the captives, recovery of sight to the blind, freedom to the oppressed, and to proclaim the jubilee of God (Luke 4:18-19).

Acts of justice are always the most difficult for Covenant Discipleship groups to understand and practice. One problem is that justice is so often equated with crime and punishment. Christians rightfully do not see why they should participate in that form of justice. Another reason groups are hesitant to name or practice acts of justice is that the problems are so large they question the value of their efforts. People frequently ask what difference they could possibly make.

This is why acts of justice are always social. Yes, each of us is only one person. But we are not alone. Each of us is one among many who are witnessing to Jesus Christ and his justice, mercy, and truth.

Writing a letter to elected representatives, signing petitions, volunteering to serve, being an informed voter, resisting the temptation to remain silent when confronted with injustice are examples of acts of justice. Christians are baptized to serve with Christ in the world: feeding hungry people, giving clean water to the thirsty, welcoming the outcast, sheltering the vulnerable, caring for the sick, and visiting prisoners. Christians are also baptized to ask why people are hungry, thirsty, and excluded and lack access to health care and why so many are imprisoned. When we ask why, we begin to move toward God's justice, which requires that all people have what they need to fully live and participate in the world.

"Under the Guidance of the Holy Spirit"

The concluding phrase of the General Rule of Discipleship tells us that "witness[ing] to Jesus Christ in the world and follow[ing] his teachings through acts of compassion, justice, worship, and devotion" are possible only by the guiding presence and power of the Holy Spirit. Discipleship is dependence upon grace. The Holy Spirit opens the heart and mind to Christ and his grace. Only grace leads us to Christ and keeps us with him. The Holy Spirit is at work in us, helping us follow Jesus in the world through promptings and warnings that "provoke [us] to love and good deeds" (Heb. 10:24).

The Holy Spirit is the third person of the Trinity. Jesus describes the Spirit's work in John 14:15-17 and 26: "If you love me, you will keep my commandments. And I will ask the Father, and he will give you another Advocate, to be with you forever. This is the Spirit of truth, whom the world cannot receive, because it neither sees him nor knows him. You know him, because he abides with you, and he will be in you. . . . But the Advocate, the Holy Spirit, whom the Father will send in my name, will teach you everything, and remind you of all that I have said to you." The word translated in the New Revised Standard Version Bible as "Advocate" is the Greek word *Paraclete*. It may also be translated as "Comforter," "Counselor," or "Helper." Jesus tells his disciples that following his death, resurrection, and ascension to the Father they will not be left alone. The Holy Spirit will be with them. He is the presence of Christ in them, serving as advocate, comforter, and guide. The Spirit will be their teacher, reminding them of all Jesus taught and equipping them to proclaim and live his good news of God's reign of love, righteousness, and justice for the world.

The Holy Spirit is, therefore, Christ's presence working in the disciple to remind us of his commands to love God with all our heart, soul, and mind, love our neighbor as ourselves, and love our fellow disciples as Christ loves. As the Spirit reminds us of the commands, the Spirit also supplies the grace we need to obey. As we cooperate with that grace to obey all of Jesus' commands, grace flows through us for others and for the world. We become a channel of God's love. As love flows through us, the Holy Spirit heals our sin-damaged heart, restoring the image of God to wholeness. New heart habits, or holy tempers, are formed as our character reflects that of Jesus: love, joy, peace, patience, kindness, generosity, faithfulness, gentleness, and self-control (Gal. 5:22-23a). This is what Wesley calls "holiness of heart and life," the goal of the Christian life.

Conclusion

The General Rule of Discipleship is a simple guide for the Christian life that serves to remind disciples of the essential practices required of those who accept the challenge of Jesus to "deny themselves, take up their cross daily, and follow me" (Luke 9:23). It aims to help disciples keep Christ at the center of all they do, in their home, workplace, recreation, and the church. As they keep Christ at the center, "faithful disciples follow the teachings *about* Jesus no less than the teachings *of* Jesus."[16]

The General Rule of Discipleship aims to help disciples maintain balance between both works of piety *and* works of mercy, both the personal *and* the social practices of Christian discipline. It serves to remind us that loving God (works of piety) compels Christians to love those whom God loves (works of mercy). Charles Wesley beautifully summarizes the outcome of the life described by the General Rule:

Let us plead for faith alone,
Faith which by our works is shown;
God it is who justifies,
Only faith the grace applies.
Active faith that lives within,
Conquers hell and death and sin,
Hallows whom it first made whole,
Forms the Savior in the soul.

Let us for this faith contend,
Sure salvation is the end;
Heaven already is begun,
Everlasting life is won.
Only let us persevere
Till we see our Lord appear,
Never from the Rock remove,
Saved by faith with works by love.[17]

The General Rule is not proscriptive or prescriptive. It is open and inclusive, welcoming to all where they are, as they are. It does not tell us what to do or not do. Rather, the General Rule points toward Jesus and provides guidance for the Christian life by reminding us of his teachings and how to do them (Matt. 7:24-27; Luke

6:46-49). It serves as a guide for living the baptismal covenant and growing in holiness of heart and life; loving God with all our heart, soul, and mind and loving our neighbor as ourselves.

> As human beings living in the world, our first consideration must be to pattern our lives according to our human role model, Jesus Christ. The Holy Spirit will then give us whatever power we need to sustain us. If this sequence is reversed, it is not long before we stumble into the pitfall of self-preoccupation. To commit ourselves to Jesus Christ and place him at the center of our congregational life means that we go with him into the world, joining him in ministry to his little ones. As we do so, we are affirmed and empowered by the Holy Spirit, who is already there ahead of us. And through the mystical union of the God who is three-in-one, we find ourselves in ministry to Christ himself among the hungry, the thirsty, the strangers, the naked, the sick, and the imprisoned (Matt. 25:35-36). But if we place the Holy Spirit at the center of our congregational life and work, seeking the grace and the power of God before we even attempt to follow the teachings of Jesus, then we begin to covet the benefits of discipleship before fulfilling our obligations.
>
> —David Lowes Watson
> *Forming Christian Disciples*, pp. 46–47

CHAPTER 3

Forming Pillars for Mission: Covenant Discipleship Groups

> So then you are no longer strangers and aliens, but you are citizens with the saints and also members of the household of God, built upon the foundation of the apostles and prophets, with Christ Jesus himself as the cornerstone. In him the whole structure is joined together and grows into a holy temple in the Lord; in whom you also are built together spiritually into a dwelling-place for God.
>
> —Ephesians 2:19-22

Have you ever visited a Gothic cathedral? Many of the most famous and beautiful cathedrals in the world were built in the Gothic style. I am most familiar with Salisbury Cathedral in Salisbury, England. I visit the city annually when I lead the Wesley Pilgrimage in England. Sarum College, which is located in the cathedral close, serves as the base for the pilgrimage. Salisbury Cathedral is a beautiful house of worship with the tallest Gothic spire in Britain.

The pointed arch is the distinctive characteristic of Gothic architecture. It allowed medieval architects to build tall, spacious

Salisbury Cathedral, England; photo by Steven W. Manskar

buildings with large windows that let in lots of light. The pointed arch distributes the weight of the building downward onto pillars. The pillars rather than the walls support the building, which is why many pillars are needed throughout a Gothic cathedral.

Imagine your congregation is like a Gothic cathedral reaching upward, toward God. Each part of the building contributes to the congregation's mission. Members of the church are like the walls, ceiling, windows, paraments, and so on. All of them have a job to do and are supported by the people who serve as the pillars. These are the "apostles and prophets" Paul mentions in Ephesians 2:20. Jesus is the keystone of the arches that holds the pillars and the church together, allowing it to be faithful to its mission of glorifying God and representing his kingdom to the world.

In Ephesians 4:11-12, Paul expands the list of the people (pillars) the congregation needs to faithfully carry out its mission in the world: "The gifts he gave were that some would be apostles, some prophets, some evangelists, some pastors, and teachers, to equip the saints for the work of ministry, for building up the body of Christ." The church needs to equip, call, deploy, and support women and men God has placed in every congregation to serve in these essential roles. They are the pillars that hold up the church. They are the disciples who help the church cooperate with the Holy Spirit in making disciples of Jesus Christ for the transformation of the world. In the Wesleyan tradition, class leaders served as the apostles, prophets, evangelists, pastors, and teachers who equip the people called Methodists for the work of ministry for building up the body of Christ. Class meetings were an effective way to surround people with a community of love and forgiveness that encouraged growing trust of God and equipped them to join Christ and his mission.

Pillars from the Past: The Class Meeting

John Wesley discovered an effective way to surround people with a community of love and forgiveness that encouraged growing trust of God and equipped them to join Christ and his mission. He knew from scripture, tradition, experience, and reason that people first need to hear the good news of Jesus Christ. They need to know and experience God's love for them revealed in the life, death, and resurrection of God's Son. People need to know God accepts them as they are, forgives their sins, and desires to heal them. God loves them and welcomes them with open arms into God's home.

John Wesley knew that people are most likely to experience God's love and acceptance in the more intimate setting of a small group. The relationships formed with other Christians when they gather weekly to pray, sing hymns, and "watch over one another in love" build the trust and intimacy people need to allow the Holy Spirit to open their heart to grace.

The class meeting was such a group. All Methodists were required to meet weekly with their class, in the care of a class leader. Group membership was twelve to fifteen women and men who lived in the same neighborhood. They met weekly. Meetings were one hour. The leader conducted the meeting. He or she opened with prayer and then gave his or her response to the question that guided each meeting: How does your soul prosper? (Or, how is it with your soul?) The General Rules provided the outline for how each member of the class gave her or his account. Members shared, one at a time, how they witnessed to Jesus Christ in the world by doing no harm and avoiding evil; by doing good to others, to their bodies and to their souls; and by practicing works of piety (the public worship of God, the ministry of the Word, the Lord's Supper, private and family prayer, searching the scriptures, and fasting or abstinence). After the leader concluded his account, he or she led the group in singing a hymn. Prayer followed the hymn, and the leader invited one class member to give his or her account in the same manner. The process was repeated for each person (prayer, account of discipleship shaped by the General Rules, and hymn).

The leader served as a role model, teacher, and friend. He or she was selected by Wesley, or the local society leaders, because he or she exhibited spiritual maturity and could be trusted with the care and nurture of souls. The class leader's role was to help members of the class to learn and to live the Christian life through teaching, exhortation, and correction in love. Wesley described their job in the General Rules:

1. To see each person in his or her class once a week at least, in order
    a. to inquire how their souls prosper;
    b. to advise, reprove, comfort or exhort, as occasion may require;
    c. to receive what they are willing to give toward the relief of the preachers, church, and poor.
2. To meet the ministers and the stewards of the society once a week, in order
    a. to inform the minister of any that are sick, or of any that walk disorderly and will not be reproved;
    b. to pay the stewards what they have received of their several classes in the week preceding.[1]

The class leader served as spiritual guide and friend to members of his or her class.

The Methodist class meeting was where the vast majority of people experienced the love, nurture, and accountability that enabled them to experience justification. The love and trust characteristic of the class meeting provided the fertile soil that nurtured faith and growth in holiness of heart and life. (To learn more about the class meeting see *The Early Methodist Class Meeting: Its Origins and Significance* by David Lowes Watson.)

The people learned Jesus' teachings in the preaching they heard each week in their parish church and the Methodist society meetings. The weekly class meeting was where they received the love and support they needed to practice Jesus' teachings in their daily lives. The relationships formed in the class meeting, with the weekly accountability for living the Christian life, was how the people called Methodists "professed to pursue holiness of heart and life, inward and outward conformity in all things to the revealed will of God; who place religion in an uniform resemblance of the great object of it; in a steady imitation of Him they worship, in all his imitable perfections; more particularly, in justice, mercy, and truth, or universal love filling the heart, and governing the life."[2]

Today, Covenant Discipleship groups form the pillars the church needs to support its mission of making disciples of Jesus Christ for the transformation of the world. These groups provide the mutual accountability and support for discipleship people need to discern God's call to serve as leaders for the church's mission. Some will answer God's call to the work of a class leader.

Pillars Today: Covenant Discipleship Groups

A Covenant Discipleship group is a small group of Christians who are ready to be accountable for their discipleship. The ideal group size is between five and seven people. The group agrees to meet weekly for one hour. The purpose of the meeting is to "watch over one another in love" by each member giving an account of how he or she witnessed to Jesus Christ in the world and followed his teachings through acts of compassion, justice, worship, and devotion under the guidance of the Holy Spirit. The meeting agenda is a covenant written by the group, shaped by the General Rule of Discipleship.

The purpose of the weekly meeting is mutual accountability and support for growing in holiness of heart and life by living the Christian life, described by John Wesley as "universal love filling the heart and governing the life" and "having the mind of Christ and walking just as he walked."

Covenant Discipleship groups are mission focused. Their mission is to help each member become a better, more dependable disciple of Jesus Christ. The weekly meeting serves as a time to take a compass heading and an opportunity to help one another make any needed course corrections. Mutual accountability helps members make sure they are following Jesus in the world and not going off on detours or dead ends. The mission focus on discipleship, with the covenant as the agenda, keeps the conversation on track. The goal is to help each other grow in holiness of heart and life by obeying Jesus' command to "love one another as I have loved you."

Meeting Agenda

Each Covenant Discipleship group writes a covenant shaped by the General Rule of Discipleship: "To witness to Jesus Christ in the world, and to follow his teachings through acts of compassion, justice, worship, and devotion under the guidance of the Holy Spirit." In the covenant, the group names the practices members are willing and able to integrate into their lives and commits to giving an account each week of what they have done, and not done. The covenant also serves as the agenda for the weekly meeting. Chapter 4 describes the purpose and content of the covenant in more detail and includes guidelines and a process for writing one.

The leader opens each group meeting with prayer followed by unison reading of the covenant preamble. She begins by giving her account of how she kept the first covenant clause. The leader and other members can ask questions as each member gives his or her account of each covenant clause. The questions are intended to help the members grow in discipleship. "Accountability" simply refers to a member giving his account of what he has done, or not done, with regard to the group's covenant.

The leader facilitates the flow of conversation guided by the agenda of the covenant. The leader manages the time, making sure the meeting begins and ends on time and ensuring that all members have time within the hour to give their account of each part of the covenant. This means the leader needs to make sure no one monopolizes the meeting time.

Shared Group Leadership

Leadership of the group is shared. Members take turns leading the meeting from week to week. Because the mission of Covenant Discipleship groups is forming members as leaders in discipleship, the shared leadership of the meetings accustoms each member to serving as a leader. To ensure time is not wasted at the beginning of meetings waiting for someone to volunteer to lead, the group needs to know who is leading the next meeting before they leave the room at the end of a meeting.

Confidentiality

Over time, the group develops an atmosphere of trust, which contributes to deeper accountability to one another. Building trust within the group draws members closer to one another and enables greater openness to receiving and giving accountability and support. As members grow closer to one another they also grow closer to God, and as a result, grow in holiness and the congregation grows leaders in discipleship.

Commitment to confidentiality is essential to building the trust necessary for the group to function well. Group members must commit to honoring the group and one another by promising to keep what is shared in the group to themselves. Members must not repeat anything said in a group meeting, no matter how innocuous, with anyone outside the group. For example, my wife knows everyone in my Covenant Discipleship group. One man in the group has two sons about the same age as our son. At the beginning of the meeting we frequently share news about what our boys are up to. At the end of the day at the dinner table, I am tempted to tell my wife the news about my friend's sons. But then I remember he told me the news in our Covenant Discipleship group meeting. I respect my friend and the group too much to jeopardize that relationship by telling my wife what he shared about his boys at the beginning of the meeting. If my wife ran into him and repeated the news he shared with me, he is likely to remember he told me that news at the beginning of our group meeting. He might then wonder what else I may have told my wife. Breaking that confidence could then damage our relationship.

Build Up the Group

Confidentiality contributes to group cohesion, as does giving a weekly account of the covenant in a way that builds up the group. Do not use the covenant as though it were a checklist. Rather, the covenant clauses serve as prompts for members to tell a story about what they did, how they experienced grace, and how they felt. Members give their account of each clause of the covenant in a way that helps at least one person in the room.

For example, like many people, my prayer life gets stale. During these times of *acedia* I typically stop praying.[3] I come up with excuses for avoiding prayer. I've learned from experience that what helps me get through such dry periods is to pray the historic prayers of the church. I typically turn to *The Book of Common Prayer* and read the daily offices of morning and evening prayer found there. Several years ago I received a copy of a new collection of prayers, *Praying in the Wesleyan Spirit: 52 Prayers for Today*, written by my friend Paul Chilcote. Paul summarized John Wesley's standard sermons (1–52) in the form of prayers. Each prayer-sermon is accompanied by a couple of stanzas of a Charles Wesley hymn. I began praying the prayers written by Paul and found it to be a rich experience. I prayed the same prayer each day for a week.

I shared with my Covenant Discipleship group how the Chilcote book helped me get back on track with daily prayer and Bible reading. One of our members was working as the youth pastor for a large United Methodist congregation. For several weeks, as she gave her account of the covenant clause in which we committed to daily scripture reading and prayer, including praying for the group member, she confessed to being so busy with work that she did not have time to read the Bible or pray. The week after I gave my account of using the Chilcote book to help restore my daily prayer practice, the youth pastor told us that my account prompted her to get a copy of the book and begin using it each day. It helped her begin spending at least a few minutes a day in prayer. My account of finding a way to get through a period of *acedia* helped another member of my group overcome her difficulty finding time to pray each day.

Covenant Discipleship Groups Are Not a Program

Covenant Discipleship is a way of life, not an educational program! Such programs are typically short-term and designed to convey information to participants. Educational programs are important to the congregation's ministry of catechesis.[4] Typically they are four to twelve weeks during which participants read a book, view videos, and discuss topics ranging from Christian theology to contemporary social issues.

By contrast, Covenant Discipleship equips Christians to live the baptismal covenant. Discipleship is not a program. It is a lifelong commitment to living the Christian life. Covenant Discipleship is an open-ended commitment because Christians never outgrow their need for accountability and support for the pursuit of holiness of heart and life.

Covenant Discipleship is part of the congregation's disciple-making foundation. Remember the illustration of the congregation being like a Gothic cathedral supported by the pillars and pointed arches. Covenant Discipleship groups form the pillars the congregation needs to carry out its mission of making disciples of Jesus Christ for the transformation of the world. The groups are where the "foundation of the apostles and prophets" is formed and maintained (Eph. 2:20).

Open to Everyone Ready to Be Accountable for Discipleship

While the groups are open to everyone in the congregation, they are for members who are ready to be accountable for living the Christian life. This is typically 15 to 20 percent of the congregation. From this group Christ will raise up class leaders, teachers, prophets, and apostles the congregation needs to equip members to join Christ in his mission in the world.

Leaders in discipleship have always been a minority. Look at the ministry of Jesus. The Gospel writers tell us that large crowds of people came to him for many reasons. He had compassion on them and loved all of them. And he asked nothing of them. But he required much from the few he called to follow him: "Let them deny themselves and take up their cross daily and follow me" (Luke 9:23). Their cross is obedience to Jesus' commands to love the Lord your God with all your heart, and with all your soul, and with all your mind," to "love your neighbor as yourself; and to love one another as I love you (Matt. 22:37-39; John 13:34-35). Those few he called gave themselves wholly to Jesus and his way of life. He equipped them to go and disciple others in his way of life. The mission of Covenant Discipleship is to form "the apostles and prophets" who are the foundation of the church's mission. They are the disciples who lead and make disciples of Jesus Christ for the transformation of the world.

Conclusion

Covenant Discipleship groups are a proven and effective way of ensuring that members of the congregation who hear Jesus' words are equipped to act on them (Matt. 7:24-29; Luke 6:46-49). They create the foundation of the congregation's missional process of making disciples of Jesus Christ equipped to join his mission in the world. The women and men who answer Christ's call to discipleship in Covenant Discipleship groups will be formed as leaders in discipleship. They become disciples who make disciples. Some will be called to the office of class leader.

Meeting weekly for one hour of mutual accountability and support for living the Christian life creates an atmosphere of trust and sharing. The trust built among group members creates a bond, which the apostle Paul referred to as *agape*, or self-giving, self-emptying love. As Christians learn and practice this form of love, they become more and more the persons God created them to be, in the image of Christ.

One of the early desert fathers, Dorotheos of Gaza, described the way humans grow closer to God:

> Suppose we were to take a compass and insert the point and draw the outline of a circle. The center point is the same distance from any point on the circumference. . . . Let us suppose that this circle is the world and that God himself is the center: the straight lines drawn from the circumference to the center are the lives of human beings. . . . Let us assume for the sake of analogy that to move toward God, then, human beings move from the circumference along the various radii of the circle to the center. But at the same time, the closer they are to God, the closer they become to one another; and the closer they are to one another, the closer they become to God.[5]

Meeting weekly with fellow followers of Jesus Christ to give an account of what we have done, and not done draws us closer to our fellow disciples. As we grow in love and trust of our sisters and brothers in Christ, we grow closer to God, who made each of us and who provides the means for each one of us to become fully the person he created us to be. As we become more and more the people God created us to be, we are equipped to join Christ's mission in the world and to serve as witnesses to him and leaders in discipleship in the congregation Christ calls us to serve.

> Of all the "commonsense" virtues of the class meeting, mutual accountability is the most important. We know-what it is like to be around people whose schedule runs like clockwork, whose homes are immaculate, who seem to find their work effortless, who are involved with community projects, who never lack the time for issues of social justice, and who are always, infuriatingly, correct. There is an aura of unreality about them. They seem to be super-human, and in an altogether different league.
>
> By contrast, most of us find it difficult to get organized for anything other than day-to-day survival. This is why the idea of mutual accountability—of joining with other people of like mind and purpose in order to make our discipleship more effective—is so logical. It is not so much a recipe for success as it is just plain, practical common sense.
>
> —David Lowes Watson
> *Covenant Discipleship*, p. 69

CHAPTER 4

The Covenant: Agenda for Discipleship

Each Covenant Discipleship group writes a covenant that is shaped by the General Rule of Discipleship. The purpose of the covenant is to help group members follow Jesus in the world where they live, work, and play. Through prayer, discernment, listening, and negotiation, the group crafts a document that serves as a guide for their pursuit of holiness of heart and life. The covenant describes the means of grace (acts of compassion, justice, worship, and devotion) everyone in the group is willing and able to practice. Once written, the covenant then serves as the agenda for the group's weekly meeting. When the group meets, each person gives an account of what he or she has done in light the covenant.

The Purpose: Growth in Christian Maturity

The purpose of the covenant is to help group members grow in Christian maturity and to provide accountability and support for following Jesus and not what is culturally popular. Maturity in faith, hope, and love are the goals of the process. The covenant reinforces that the weekly group meeting is not where members' discipleship happens. Rather, it is where they show up week after week after week to make sure discipleship happens during the other hours of the week.

The covenant is a means to the group's pursuit of holiness of heart and life, or what John Wesley calls perfection in love (1 John 2:3-6).

Other words for this type of perfection are *full grown*, *adult*, *of full age*, and *mature*. This notion brings to mind Ephesians 4:14-16: "We must no longer be children, tossed to and fro and blown about by every wind of doctrine, by people's trickery, by their craftiness in deceitful scheming. But speaking the truth in love, we must grow up in every way into him who is the head, into Christ, from whom the whole body, joined and knit together by every ligament with which it is equipped, as each part is working properly, promotes the body's growth in building itself up in love." In these few verses the apostle Paul describes the goal of the Christian life.

John Wesley described the process of growth from infancy to maturity in Sermon 45, "The New Birth." He said it is similar to physical birth and growth. While a child is in the mother's womb it has eyes but cannot see. It has ears but hearing is muffled and distorted. After it travels down the birth canal and is born into the world, its eyes and ears are opened. The baby is able for the first time to see and hear the world as it is. In a similar way, when the baby comes to faith in Christ, it is born anew and its spiritual eyes and ears are opened:

> He feels "the love of God shed abroad in his heart by the Holy Ghost which is given unto him." And all his spiritual senses are then "exercised to discern" spiritual "good and evil." By the use of these he is daily increasing in the knowledge of God, of Jesus Christ whom he hath sent, and of all the things pertaining to his inward kingdom. And now he may properly be said to live: God having quickened him by his Spirit, he is alive to God through Jesus Christ. He lives a life which the world knoweth not of, a "life" which "is hid with Christ in God." God is continually breathing, as it were, upon his soul, and his soul is breathing unto God. Grace is descending into his heart, and prayer and praise ascending to heaven. And by this intercourse between God and man, this fellowship with the Father and the Son, as by a kind of spiritual respiration,

the life of God in the soul is sustained: and the child of God grows up, till he comes to "the full measure of the stature of Christ."[1]

The group covenant plays an important role in helping Christians cooperate with grace and the Holy Spirit to grow in the holiness God seeks for them. The covenant is a means to the goal of maturity, to becoming a full-grown, fully formed, adult Christian who is a channel of grace for the world and the church.

A Living Document

The covenant is a living document. Because its purpose is to help the group and its members grow in holiness, it must be adjusted to meet the group's spiritual needs. This is why groups should evaluate their covenant at least annually and, if needed, revise it.

If the group habitually neglects a practice named in the covenant, then it should be discarded and replaced with a practice everyone is really willing and able to do and to be accountable for each week. Or the group could revise such a practice to make it something the group will do. If a practice has become routine, then the group could revise it to make it more challenging. For example, "We will read the Bible and pray every day" could be revised to read, "We will read the Bible and pray for at least thirty minutes every day." This revision maintains the central disciplines of daily Bible reading and prayer and makes it more specific, in that each member commits to devoting at least thirty minutes a day, leaving it up to each person to decide how to put into practice.

A suggested process for revising a covenant can be found in appendix C on page 193.

Three Essential Sections

The covenant has three sections, the preamble, the clauses, and the conclusion. Each section serves an important function in the covenant and the life of the group. Completing each section is essential, because members come to a deeper understanding of the covenant, the group, themselves, and the group's role in the church's mission.

The Preamble

The preamble states the nature and purpose of the covenant. The covenant serves as a compass that keeps members on course with Jesus in the world. Its purpose is to keep group members mindful of how they intend to grow in holiness of heart and life through obeying Jesus' teachings. The covenant aims to keep their hearts open to the grace they need to love God with all their heart, soul, and mind and to love their neighbors as themselves. It also reminds them of the commandment Jesus gave his friends at their last supper: "I give you a new commandment, that you love one another. Just as I have loved you, you also should love one another. By this everyone will know that you are my disciples, if you have love for one another" (John 13:34-35). The covenant and the dynamic of mutual accountability and support in the weekly meetings enable the group to love one another. Their love for one another contributes to their witness to Jesus in the community of the church and in the world.

The preamble makes clear the covenant is not a set of regulations. The covenant is a guide for how group members intend to follow the way of Jesus in their daily lives. It is not meant to cause guilt or shame. The covenant reminds members that the group meeting is not where their discipleship happens, it's where they show up week after week to make sure that it happens; that they are making their best effort to live as witnesses to Jesus Christ in the world by obeying all of his teachings, not only the ones they like.

The preamble emphasizes the group's dependence upon grace. John Wesley taught that grace is the presence and power of God working in the world to redeem and restore humankind and all creation to wholeness. Grace is the self-emptying, self-giving love revealed in the life, death, and resurrection of Jesus Christ. Grace is the power of God's love that gives new birth (John 3:3; 2 Cor. 5:17) and faith, a restored relationship with God the Father through the Son, Jesus Christ (Eph. 2:8-10). Faith and grace help us cooperate with the Holy Spirit, who overcomes the power of sin in us and forms holy tempers, habits and attitudes aligned with the way of Jesus: love, joy, peace, patience, kindness, generosity, faithfulness, gentleness, and self-control (Gal. 5:22-23).

When we cooperate with grace, the way of Jesus becomes our new way of life and we become "ambassadors for Christ" in the world (2 Cor. 5:16-21). When Covenant Discipleship groups meet to pray and to give their weekly accounts of how they walked with Jesus in the world, the stories remind members of the presence and power of grace at work in one another and in the world. The weekly meeting reminds them of their dependence upon grace as they follow and witness to Jesus Christ in the world.

Finally, the preamble is a statement of shared faith in Christ. Faith is more than agreeing with creeds or doctrines. It is more than saying, "Jesus Christ is my personal Savior." Believing is essential, but it is only the beginning of faith. Wesley taught that faith is belief that shapes our life in the world. Notice that I said life in the world and not life in the church. Faith certainly influences our life in the church; the way we relate to sisters and brothers in Christ and participate in the life and mission of the congregation are important fruits of faith. But more significant is how our faith compels us to behave in the world God loves and Christ is working to redeem.

This means that faith is primarily a relationship with the crucified and risen Son of God whose name is Jesus of Nazareth. Faith describes the nature of our relationship with him. It means we believe and trust his teachings and promises. Believing and trusting his teachings leads to applying them to our life in the world: our home, workplace, and recreation. Faith in Christ opens our heart to his grace, making it possible for the Holy Spirit to inspire and lead us to obey his teachings and live as a channel of God's love for the world.

Shared faith in Christ leads the group to understand the group's aim is to assist the congregation in faithfully carrying out its mission to make disciples of Jesus Christ for the transformation of the world.

Faith in Christ helps the group know that their covenant belongs to the congregation, because the group is an important part of the congregation's mission. While faith is deeply personal, it is not private. I say this because faith is at the center of the baptismal covenant, which is a public declaration of faith in Christ and a commitment to serve with him and the church in the world. The public nature of faith in Christ is why the group's covenant belongs to the group, the congregation, and to God.

The covenant preamble states the nature and purpose of the covenant, makes clear the covenant is not a set of regulations, emphasizes the group's dependence upon grace, and is a statement of shared faith in Christ. It sets the ground rules for the group's life. It is a good idea for the preamble to include practical statements such as "We will show up each week, unless prevented. If a member cannot attend a meeting he or she will notify the group before the next meeting. We will participate fully by listening, asking questions, and offering encouragement and correction to help fellow members grow in discipleship as we watch over one another in love."

Covenant Clauses

The clauses describe the means of grace everyone in the group is willing and able to habitually practice as they strive to follow all of Jesus' teachings. The covenant includes at least one clause describing acts of compassion, acts of justice, acts of worship, and acts of devotion. The clauses are listed in the same order as their corresponding category appears in the General Rule of Discipleship. This means that the acts of compassion and acts of justice appear before the acts of worship and acts of devotion.

The order does not imply that works of mercy are more important than works of piety. Both are equally essential in the Christian life. Placing the works of mercy early in the list of clauses is a wise approach, because experience tells us that acts of justice make many Christians uncomfortable. This is why many Covenant Discipleship groups place them at the bottom of their covenant. When the hour allotted for the meeting is up, they expect the group will not have time to account for their acts of justice.

John Wesley believed works of mercy are means of grace, and at times even more so than the works of piety:

> But he should be more zealous for the ordinances of Christ than for the Church itself; for prayer in public and private; for the Lord's Supper; for reading, hearing, and meditating on his word; and for the much-neglected duty of fasting. These he should earnestly recommend; first, by his example; and then by advice, by argument, persuasion, and exhortation, as often as occasion offers.
>
> Thus should he show his zeal for works of piety; but much more for works of mercy; seeing "God will have mercy and not sacrifice"; that is, rather than sacrifice. Whenever, therefore, one interferes with the other, works of mercy are to be preferred. Even reading, hearing, prayer, are to be omitted, or to be postponed, "at charity's almighty call"; when we are called to relieve the distress of our neighbor, whether in body or soul.[2]

Acts of compassion and justice are how Christians live out their love of God through loving those whom God loves. Therefore, the works of mercy come before the works of piety in the General Rule of Discipleship and in the group's covenant.

Balance

The group covenant must include at least one clause in each of the four practices: compassion, justice, worship, and devotion. Maintaining balance ensures the group will attend to all of Jesus' teachings and not limit themselves to those they are temperamentally inclined to follow. Balanced discipleship shaped by the General Rule of Discipleship encourages members to get outside their comfort zones as they take on practices that are challenging to them. When in faith we go to those unfamiliar places and people, we need to remember that Christ is waiting to meet us there. When we go to places and people that make us feel uncomfortable, we are more dependent upon and vulnerable to the power of grace. Habitually getting outside our comfort zones allows us to experience grace's power to enlarge our heart and grow in holiness.

Acts of Compassion

Acts of compassion are the acts of kindness we do for a neighbor who is suffering or in need of help. Our neighbor is anyone anywhere in the world. The baptismal covenant tells us that disciples of Jesus Christ "serve as Christ's representatives in the world."[3] Scripture tells us Jesus habitually responded with compassion for people he encountered. He fed the hungry. He healed the sick. He comforted people who were mourning.

Disciples of Jesus are commissioned by him to imitate him. This means Christians respond with kindness and love when we encounter people who are poor, homeless, lonely, hungry, mourning, or sick. Christians visit prisoners in jail. We care for those who are sick and homebound.

Acts of compassion are the *personal* works of mercy. They are acts of kindness we do with persons we encounter at home, work, school, on the street, in airports, on the road. I once heard the writer and humorist Tom Bodett tell a story he called something like "The Club for People Who Notice." He was in a grocery store checkout line one day when he noticed the person at the front of the line was a young mom with a couple of small children. The mom realized she did not have enough money to pay for the groceries she needed. Bodett noticed the woman in line behind the mom was paying attention to the young woman's plight. She went to the mom and offered to pay what was needed to cover the deficit. The relief in the mom's face was priceless. Bodett concludes the story by saying the woman who helped the mom in that grocery checkout line was a member of the Club for People Who Notice (or something like that). He said he wants to be in that club, and that the world would be a much better place if more people made the effort to join in.

The baptismal covenant tells us that Christians are called to be members of the "Club." The church is called to train its members to be people who notice the people in their neighborhood and habitually respond to them with the same compassion Jesus taught his disciples.

Acts of Justice

While Christians are under orders to care for their neighbors who are poor, hungry, thirsty, homeless, sick, and imprisoned, we are also called by Christ to ask why. In the baptismal covenant Christians promise to "accept the freedom and power God gives you to resist evil, injustice, and oppression in whatever forms they present themselves."[4] The General Rule of Discipleship and our Covenant Discipleship group, guided by the acts of justice in our group's covenant, help us keep this promise.

Acts of justice are the *social or public* works of mercy. They are action Christians take together to address the causes of our neighbor's suffering. Acts of justice are frequently related to acts of compassion. While compassion is the personal act of kindness that alleviates the need of an individual, acts of justice are how Christians respond as a group or community with other people of faith to address the systems and institutions that are the cause of the neighbor's suffering.

Acts of Worship

The first three practices John Wesley listed in the third General Rule are acts of worship: the public worship of God, the ministry of the Word, and the Supper of the Lord. The one thing these have in common is that Christians do them together. They cannot be done alone, in private. They are expressions of the church's devotion to the triune God. One characteristic of the Christian life is gathering with fellow Christians to offer ourselves in service to God and to build one another up through praise, prayer, scripture, proclamation, confession, forgiveness, sacrament, and sending. Worship is like breathing. In worship the church opens itself to receive the grace and power we need to faithfully witness to Jesus Christ and join his mission in the world.

Acts of Devotion

The second three practices in the third General Rule are acts of devotion: family and private prayer, searching the scriptures, and fasting or abstinence. They are means of grace we practice daily in private to cultivate personal relationship with Christ. Acts of devotion are the various ways we open ourselves to grace when we are alone with Christ. They are practices we do every day to keep in touch with him and listen to him so that we can follow him each day at work, at school, on the road, and at home. Like acts of worship, acts of devotion keep us centered in Christ. They equip us to live each day as his faithful witnesses in the world.

Promptings and Warnings of the Holy Spirit

The group covenant includes at least one clause that acknowledges promptings and warnings of the Holy Spirit. This clause says members of the Covenant Discipleship group will be open and aware of the leading of the Holy Spirit who is working in the group and its members and in the world. Promptings lead us to act positively with a person or situation we encounter during our day. Warnings lead us to avoid situations or actions that are contrary to love and justice.

Let me share an example of what I mean. One evening as we were preparing supper, my wife noticed we were low on milk. So I drove to the local grocery store and bought the milk, and as I was getting into my car to go home, a man approached me. He smiled as he asked if I could drive him to a truck stop near downtown Nashville. He explained that his sister worked at the restaurant and was expecting him. The problem was that his car had broken down. The guy said he would give me ten dollars if I would drive him to his sister. My normal response would be to politely decline such a request. My wife was waiting for me to come home for dinner and to bring the milk for our son. Also, I would never let a stranger into my car. I never pick up hitchhikers for that reason.

But something was different here. Something very clearly told me, "This man is telling the truth. He is safe. Give him a ride so he can be with his sister." So I told the man, "Get in. I know the place you're talking about. It's about ten miles from here." A great sense of relief, and a little disbelief, came over the man's face. He thanked me and slid into the passenger seat.

As we rode west on I-40 toward Nashville, I learned he had gone to a bar near my neighborhood to hear a friend of his play in a band. We talked about Christ and faith and forgiveness. Before we knew it, I pulled into the parking lot of the truck stop. As promised, the man's sister was pacing nervously outside the restaurant. He thanked me again and insisted on giving me the ten dollars, which I declined. I told him to get some flowers for his sister.

I arrived home about an hour later than my wife expected me. You see this happened before mobile phones, and I had no way of telling her what was happening. With a mixture of relief and frustration she asked, "What took you so long?" When I told her the story, she insisted, "Don't you ever do that again!"

As I reflected on the experience with the man who needed a ride, I believe the voice that told me "This man is telling the truth. He is safe. Give him a ride so he can be with his sister" was a prompting of the Holy Spirit. It just as easily could have warned me to get in my car and go home.

When we submit to the discipline of loving God with all our heart, soul, and mind and loving those whom God loves, our ears become more attuned to what God is up to in our life and in our neighborhood. We will be more aware of promptings and warnings of the Holy Spirit. And we will be open to the grace needed to respond accordingly.

The Conclusion

The final section of the covenant is a brief statement that reaffirms the nature and purpose of the covenant. The conclusion emphasizes once again that grace is the dynamic of discipleship. It reminds us of our dependence upon and openness to grace to live the Christian life. We need to remember that grace is given and received most frequently through relationships with people God places in our life.

The Covenant Discipleship group meeting is an opening to give and receive grace. Christ promises "where two or three are gathered in my name, I am there among you" (Matt. 18:20).

The Christian life is lived in community with others who share the same baptismal promises to walk with us in the way of Jesus. Christ comes to us in the company of other Christians who "profess to pursue holiness of heart and life."[5] The Covenant Discipleship group is a means of grace that provides the mutual accountability and support we need to follow Jesus in the world and serve him by helping the congregation equip its members to join in his mission in the world.

The conclusion to the covenant should be no more than one or two sentences. It may be written in the form of a prayer to conclude each meeting:

> Open my eyes to your presence, O God,
>   that I may see the sorrows and joys of your creatures.
> Open my ears to your will, O God,
>   that I may have the strength to keep this covenant.
> Open my heart and my hands in mercy, O God,
>   that I may receive mercy when I fail. Amen.

The content of the covenant requires the consensus of the group. Every member of the group must agree to every word on the page before it becomes the group's covenant. This requires some negotiation. Consensus begins with mutual respect for one another. Members of the group bring varying degrees of experience and maturity with discipleship. Some will have many years of experience with faith in Christ and life in the church. Others will be new to faith and the church. Others will be somewhere in between. To achieve consensus members must begin with mutual respect for what each person brings to the group. It requires prayer, listening, negotiation, and compromise. Striving for and reaching consensus is how the group is formed as a community of fellow Christians in pursuit of holiness of heart and life and leaders in discipleship for the congregation.

Covenant Writing Guidelines

In writing the covenant for a Covenant Discipleship group, consider the following guidelines.

First, *begin where you are and not where you think you should be.* A common mistake groups make when they begin to write their covenants is they include clauses that describe practices they think faithful disciples should do. But when the group begins to put the covenant into practice, they find they either cannot or do not want to engage in the practices described in their covenant.

For example, a group may include a clause such as "We will pray and read scripture an hour in the morning and at night." When the group meets to give an account of how well each member has kept the covenant, it is likely that most will report difficulty with such a clause. After three or four weeks, particularly if the group has included other clauses like this one, which are practices beyond the will and ability of members, they will give up and quit the group.

More reasonable and practicable wording for the example given above is "We will read scripture and pray every day." This allows members to enter the practice where they are. It works for the member who is ready to commit to reading scripture and praying an hour in the morning and at night. It works just as well for the member for whom daily scripture reading and prayer is new and devoting five to ten minutes a day is great progress.

It is okay to include covenant practices that members are already doing. The difference is that members will give an account of their practice each week. The weekly accountability and support will help them grow and mature in their practice of the works of piety and works of mercy.

Begin where you are and not where you think you should be. Include in the covenant only those practices everyone is willing and able to do. As the group makes progress in disciplined living of the Christian life over time, members may agree to revise the covenant to reflect that growth.

A second guideline is to *keep clauses simple and as specific as possible*. Avoid broad statements of intention, which are difficult to assess or evaluate. Keeping clauses simple and specific allows group members to more easily give an account of how they have incorporated the practices into their life. Clauses need to be practical, which means they contribute to the group member's growth in holiness of heart and life.

Third, *limit the covenant to eight to ten clauses*. The covenant should fit on one side of an 8 ½ by 11-inch sheet of paper with one-inch margins, and twelve-point Times New Roman font (or something similar). Limiting the size of the group to seven people and the length of the covenant helps the group meeting to keep within a one-hour time commitment. The covenant should be easy to memorize and practical. Balance the clauses with one or two acts of compassion, justice, worship, and devotion. The preamble is a brief paragraph. The conclusion must be no more than one or two simple sentences.

Fourth, *take as long as necessary in writing the covenant*. It is important for the covenant to reflect the character and needs of group members. This means the group must take the time needed to listen to each member as the covenant is negotiated. Be open to the various levels of experience and maturity in discipleship within the group. Members need to respect one another and be flexible and willing to compromise during the covenant writing process.

Covenant Discipleship groups typically take four to six weeks to write their covenants. Some come together faster. Some take more time. There is no deadline. A group should take as long as it needs for the group to reach consensus. But do not get bogged down in word crafting. Be open to the leading of the Holy Spirit to guide the process. The goal is to write a covenant the group can live with, one that helps members grow in discipleship and contributes to the church's mission in the world.

The clauses should reflect the context of the group. When needs arise in the community, world, or church, members may introduce clauses that enable the group to respond faithfully. Clauses may be changed or dropped as needed to ensure the covenant is relevant to the group's context.

Group members may adopt a personal clause. Group members may be prompted by the Holy Spirit to take on an act of compassion, justice, worship, or devotion in addition to the group's covenant. This is known as a personal clause. The group member shares how she is prompted by the Spirit to add the practice to her life. The member gives an account of how she has kept the personal clause during the weekly meeting. The group promises to pray for the member, that she faithfully keeps the clause and that the practice contributes to her growth in holiness.

Several years ago, in the weeks leading up to Lent, I was prompted to fast and pray one day each week of Lent. I shared the prompting with my Covenant Discipleship group, but I could not convince them to join me in the weekly fast. We agreed I would have a personal clause: "I will fast from food on Wednesday, devoting the day to prayer. The money I would have spent on food for that day will be given to Bread for the World."

During the weeks of Lent, I gave an account of my practice of fasting on Wednesdays to my Covenant Discipleship group. The group agreed to pray for me on Wednesdays. They also agreed to refrain from inviting me to join them in a meal on my fast day. The personal clause expired on Easter Sunday. I grew closer to Christ and in my knowledge of the problem of hunger in the world. The group benefited from keeping me in prayer and hearing my account of my practice of a weekly one-day fast.

As beneficial as personal clauses may be, they are an exception to the practice of Covenant Discipleship. They are intended to be limited to help address individual members' needs and promptings of the Holy Spirit. Do not create a covenant filled with personal clauses. Doing so defeats the purpose of the Covenant Discipleship group.

How to Write a Covenant with Your Group

After a Covenant Discipleship group decides when and where to hold its weekly meeting, its first task is to write the group covenant. Writing the covenant together helps members learn more about one another and produces the document that will serve as the group's agenda.

As the group begins its covenant writing process, members must agree to practice mutual respect. The process requires that members listen to one another. Because there must be consensus about every part of the covenant, members must be willing to compromise. This requires openness to negotiation. The entire process must be supported by prayer and openness to the leading of the Holy Spirit.

The covenant is shaped by the General Rule of Discipleship: "To *witness* to Jesus Christ in the world and to follow his teachings through acts of compassion, justice, worship, and devotion under the guidance of the Holy Spirit." This General Rule serves as the framework around which the covenant is built by the group. The group covenant puts flesh on the bones of the General Rule. It is a statement of how the group intends to follow Jesus Christ in the world.

This simple five-step process can help a group write its covenant:

Step 1: Holding the Introductory Meeting

The first meeting is led by the pastor or a layperson who has experience in Covenant Discipleship groups. The leader gives a brief overview of the General Rule of Discipleship and the structure of the group covenant: preamble, clauses, and conclusion. Distribute copies of this book, which can serve as a valuable guide for the group.

At the conclusion of the meeting, the leader tells the group to think and pray about the acts of compassion, justice, worship, and devotion they are willing and able to do and want included in the covenant. Each member is to bring to the next meeting four clauses: an act of compassion, an act of justice, an act of worship, and an act of devotion he or she is willing and able to practice and to give a weekly account.

Step 2: Writing the Clauses

The materials needed for this session are four pieces of newsprint, sticky notes, pens, and masking tape (to hang the newsprint on the walls around the room). At the top of each piece of newsprint write, in large letters, one of the covenant categories: COMPASSION, JUSTICE, WORSHIP, DEVOTION. Hang the newsprint sheets on the wall around the room.

Distribute sticky notes to each member of the group. You may want to have four different colors, each corresponding to the four categories of clauses: compassion, justice, worship, devotion. Instruct group members to write each clause (see step 1) on one sticky note. When they have finished writing, they place the notes on the appropriate newsprint sheet. Acts of compassion go on the sheet titled COMPASSION, acts of justice go on the sheet titled JUSTICE, and so forth.

After all members have placed their sticky notes on the four newsprint sheets, instruct everyone to go to each sheet and read all the clauses posted there. Place clauses that are very similar near one another. Repeat this process until all clauses have been sorted.

The group will find much duplication of clauses. This tells members what is important to the group. The task remaining is to edit the similar clauses into one clause. Repeat this process until the group has reached consensus on at least one clause in each of the four areas. There should be no more than two clauses in each area.

When the group has completed its clauses, instruct the group to think and pray about the covenant preamble. Each member is to bring to the next meeting a proposed preamble.

Step 3: Writing the Preamble

A process similar to the one described above is used for writing the preamble. The only difference is that only two sheets of newsprint are needed and a supply of slightly larger sticky notes.

At the beginning of the meeting, distribute large sticky notes to the group. Ask members to write the preamble they have brought to the meeting on the sticky note. When members complete their writing, each one posts his or her preamble on the sheet of newsprint. After all have posted their preambles, invite the group to silently read the collected preambles. Look for common phrases and ideas.

On a second piece of newsprint, write phrases and ideas found in the collected preambles. The group then begins editing until the preamble is completed. This will usually be finished in one meeting. If needed, finish the preamble writing at the beginning of the next meeting.

At the conclusion of the meeting that completes the writing of the covenant preamble, ask group members to bring to the next meeting a one- or two-sentence conclusion for the group covenant.

Step 4: Writing the Conclusion

The process for completing the covenant conclusion is identical to the preamble writing process (see step 3).

Step 5: Signing the Covenant

When the group has reached consensus on every part of the covenant, it is ready for everyone's signature. Print a master copy of the covenant for everyone to sign and date. A copy of the signed covenant is then distributed to each member of the group.

Give a copy of the signed and dated covenant to the pastor. In addition, post a copy on a bulletin board in the church and on the congregation's website. Making the covenant available to everyone in the congregation helps all to know that Covenant Discipleship groups are an expression of the congregation's mission of disciple making and leader formation.

Points to Note

Consider the following recommendations and reminders for writing the group's covenant:

- Have one person lead the group through the covenant-writing process. This provides continuity for the process. The ideal leader is someone who has experience participating in Covenant Discipleship groups.
- Limit the covenant to no more than ten clauses. Balance clauses between all four areas of the General Rule of Discipleship: acts of compassion, justice, worship, and devotion.
- Keep the covenant brief so that it fits on one side of a single 8 ½ by 11-inch piece of paper with one-inch margins and twelve-point font. If the covenant spills over to a second page, edit it to fit on only one page.
- Keep clauses concise and specific. This practice keeps the covenant practicable. Avoid generalized clauses, for example, "We will endeavor to oppose injustice." A better clause is "I will communicate regularly with elected officials regarding issues of justice," or "I will join Amnesty International to write letters on behalf of prisoners of conscience." Rather than make general statements, state what the group is willing and able to do to follow Jesus' teachings.
- Begin where members are, not where they think they should be. Avoid including acts of compassion, justice, worship, and devotion members think they should be doing. Rather, include only acts everyone is willing and able to do now. It is okay to include practices members are already doing. The group will help members be more disciplined in their practice, because everyone will give a weekly account.
- Place the clauses in the same order as they are named in the General Rule of Discipleship. This means the first category of clauses to appear in the covenant is acts of compassion, followed by acts of justice, worship, and devotion. This ensures that acts of justice, which are always the most difficult and frequently avoided, will remain at the top of the group agenda.
- Use a slightly modified version of this process when it is time to revise the group's covenant. Evaluate and, if needed, revise the group covenant at least once a year.

Following this simple process will help a group complete the writing of its covenant in no more than four meetings, but it's okay if you need a meeting or two more. This process ensures that everyone's voice is heard and contributes to the covenant writing process. When everyone participates equally, everyone is invested in the success of the group.

Conclusion

The scriptural meaning of covenant is to enter willingly into a binding agreement with God. It is a response to God's gracious initiative which cannot later be undone, however difficult it might be to keep. It can only be broken.

Many scholars believe that the Hebrew word for covenant, *berith,* came from an Assyrian word, meaning a *shackle* or a *fetter.* This is because the people of God in the Old Testament times learned the hard way that there is no greater captivity than to be enslaved to self-interest and self-gratification. The only true freedom is to be bound to God in faithful obedience (Exod. 19:4-5; Jer. 7:22-23). In the New Testament, this became the New Covenant of the Spirit, mediated through Jesus Christ, who himself fulfilled the law, and in whose service is perfect freedom (Acts 2:14-18; 2 Cor. 3:7-18; Gal. 5:16-18; Heb. 9:15).

The scripture makes clear, of course, that the people in Israel broke their covenant with God (Jer. 31:32; Heb. 8:9), just as the church time and again has broken the new covenant in Christ. It is a constant source of wonder that God is always faithful to these covenants even when the people of God are fickle and faithless (Jer. 31:33-34; Ezek. 16:60-63; Hos. 2:14-23; Heb. 8:6-13). Yet such has been the pattern across centuries of Jewish and Christian history.

This is why the supreme privilege of Christian discipleship is to be called into covenant, into this special relationship with the God of all creation. It is the only way we can even begin to live the sort of life God intends for us, and to avoid the slavery of self-interest and self-determination.

Thus the covenant of a covenant discipleship group is not an end in itself, and most certainly not a set of rules and regulations. Rather it is a dynamic means of grace, an instrument to help Christian disciples follow the leading of God's Spirit in the world.

—David Lowes Watson
Covenant Discipleship: Christian Formation through Mutual Accountability, pp. 113–14.

CHAPTER 5

Introducing Covenant Discipleship to the Congregation

Jesus said, "Everyone who hears these words of mine and acts on them will be like a wise man who built his house on rock."

—Matthew 7:24

Where Covenant Discipleship Fits

Covenant Discipleship groups are part of the foundation of the congregation's disciple-making mission. Covenant Discipleship is a proven and effective means of equipping the people who respond to Jesus' invitation to discipleship.

Covenant Discipleship groups are how congregations form the apostles and prophets Paul describes in Ephesians 2:20 as being the foundation of God's household. They are leaders in discipleship who work as partners with the appointed pastor to keep the promises the congregation makes in the baptismal covenant:

> With God's help we will proclaim the good news and live according to the example of Christ. We will surround these

persons with a community of love and forgiveness, that they may grow in their trust of God, and be found faithful in their service to others. We will pray for them, that they may be true disciples who walk in the way that leads to life.[1]

The mission of Covenant Discipleship groups is to provide the disciples who disciple others in the congregation and in the neighborhood. These disciples who make disciples form the foundation, the rock, upon which the congregation is built as an outpost of God's reign, centered on Christ and his mission.

Earlier in this book I quoted from Mike Breen's insightful book *Building a Discipling Culture*: "If you make disciples, you always get the church. But if you make a church, you rarely get disciples."[2] He goes on to explain that church leaders need to understand that discipleship builds the church, not the other way around. He correctly says, "We need to understand the church as the *effect* of discipleship and not the *cause*. If you set out to build the church, there is no guarantee you will make disciples. It is far more likely that you will create consumers who depend on the spiritual services that religious professionals provide."[3]

Nowhere in scripture does Christ tell his disciples to build a church. He mentions the church in only two places, Matthew 16:18 and 18:15-17. Jesus describes the job of his disciples in Matthew 28:18-20: "Jesus, undeterred, went right ahead and gave his charge: 'God authorized and commanded me to commission you: Go out and train everyone you meet, far and near, in this way of life, marking them by baptism in the threefold name: Father, Son, and Holy Spirit. Then instruct them in the practice of all I have commanded you. I'll be with you as you do this, day after day after day, right up to the end of the age.'" I'm quoting *The Message* here, because Eugene Peterson provides an accurate translation of the Greek word most commonly rendered as "make disciples." He clearly illuminates the words as meaning "train everyone you meet, far and near, in this way of life." This is the work of disciples who make disciples, and by extension, the work of the church. This is the job description of lay and clergy leaders.

Discipleship (living the Christian life) and disciple making (training others in the Christian life) is the work of the church. When disciples do their job, Jesus promises to build the church: "And I tell you, you are Peter, and on this rock I will build my church, and the gates of Hades will not prevail against it" (Matt. 16:18). Here Jesus tells Simon Peter the meaning of his name. Peter is "Rocky." His name is a play on the Greek *petros*, which means "rock." Peter is the leader of the disciples. When Jesus points to him and says, "On this rock I will build my church," he is saying he will build his church on the rock of discipleship.

This brings us back to Matthew 7:24: "Everyone then who hears these words of mine and acts on them will be like a wise man who built his house on rock." Discipleship is the rock upon which God's household, the church, is built.

A Two-Step Process

Introducing Covenant Discipleship to a congregation is a two-step process that requires planning, persistence, and leadership. The process is akin to remodeling or rebuilding a house. The clergy and lay leadership team must be supportive and involved. Covenant Discipleship is not another program offered to interested members of the congregation. It is intended to become integral to the disciple-making mission of the congregation and will involve changes to the congregation's culture over time. This means following the process will become part of the congregation's life for years into the future.

Step 1: Launching Pilot Groups

A proven method of introducing Covenant Discipleship groups in a congregation is to use pilot groups. A pilot group is a Covenant Discipleship group that meets for a year. During that year the congregation is prepared for offering ongoing discipleship groups to everyone. Members of the pilot group speak to groups such as the church council, Sunday school classes, confirmation classes, United

Inform the director of Wesleyan Leadership at Discipleship Ministries of your plans to begin Covenant Discipleship groups and class leaders in the congregation you serve. This is a valuable source of resources and support for you and the congregation as you begin this journey. Be certain to order a supply of "Covenant Discipleship Groups" brochures. Order as many as you will use. They will be sent to you free of charge. Send an e-mail to cdgroups@umcdiscipleship. org. Include the number of brochures you need, your name, congregation name, and mailing address.

The director of Wesleyan Leadership has years of experience with Covenant Discipleship and will be a valuable source of support and resources as you embark on this work.

Consider inviting the director of Wesleyan Leadership to serve as speaker or preacher and workshop leader for a Covenant Discipleship Weekend to be held at the conclusion of the pilot year. Contact the director of Wesleyan Leadership at cdgroups@umcdiscipleship.org.

Methodist Women, United Methodist Men, and United Methodist Youth Fellowship. They share their experience of weekly account-ability and support for living the Christian life, how it is a blessing, challenge, and responsibility of their baptism. The pastor regularly gives testimony about his or her experience in the Covenant Dis-cipleship group. Members may give brief testimonies during Sunday morning worship services. Key leaders of the congregation receive reports on the group's progress throughout the pilot year.

First, set a date and time for a brief Covenant Discipleship infor-mation presentation for the entire congregation. Begin recruiting with a general invitation to the congregation. Everyone needs to hear, several times, that a pilot group is forming and all are invited to learn about it. Everyone who is ready to be accountable for their disciple-ship one hour a week is welcome to participate. The general invitation is important because it sends the message that Covenant Discipleship is open to everyone. This helps members understand the groups are not exclusive or elitist. People also need to know that the group is one way the congregation is keeping the promises it makes in the baptismal covenant. The general invitation is also important because people you would never think were interested in or ready for Covenant Discipleship, but have been waiting for such an invitation to come their way, are given an opportunity to respond and participate.

Most members of the pilot group will be gathered through personal, face-to-face invitation. These are people whom you believe are ready for Covenant Discipleship, who either are leaders or potential leaders in the congregation, and people who would benefit from participation in the pilot group and will be a blessing to the congregation's mission. Look for people with bright eyes when they talk about, or hear others talk about, following Jesus and joining his mission in the world. Good candidates are persons who have completed *Disciple* Bible study or the Walk to Emmaus or both. Invite these people to attend the information session.

Plan to present the basics of Covenant Discipleship groups in the information session. Invite those who are interested in forming a pilot group to join in a study and discussion of this book. Decide on a day and time to meet for one hour. When the day and time of the pilot group meeting is decided, make sure it is also published in the congregation's weekly calendar.

Depending upon the congregation's size, there may be enough people to form as many as three pilot groups. Each group should have no more than seven people.

Once the pilot group's covenant is completed and signed, it becomes the agenda for their weekly meeting. (See chapter 4 and Appendix B for help in writing a covenant.) Make a copy of the covenant and post it in the church and on the congregation's website for members to see. Posting the group's covenant helps members of the congregation understand the group's mission. It also communicates that the group exists to serve the congregation's mission. The covenant belongs to the congregation as much as it belongs to the Covenant Discipleship group.

During the pilot year, members of the pilot Covenant Disciple-ship group meet with various groups in the congregation to share their experience. The goal is to help congregation members who may never feel called to this type of discipleship practice to understand and value its importance to the overall mission of the congregation: to make disciples of Jesus Christ for the transformation of the world.

Step 2: Opening the Groups

Plan a Covenant Discipleship Weekend to conclude the pilot year. A three-day event open to the entire congregation, it must be well planned and publicized as the culmination of the introductory year. The goal of the event is to invite people to begin new Covenant Dis-cipleship groups. It is also an opportunity to introduce the office of class leader as the next stage of Covenant Discipleship in the congregation.

The Friday Supper

The weekend begins with a Friday evening congregational meal. Invite the whole congregation to this event. Prepare and serve the food in the way that works best for your context. The meal is pri-marily an opportunity to share table fellowship. Members of the pilot group work together to serve the food and mingle among the people, spreading themselves among the tables to share with as many people as possible their experience of the Covenant Discipleship group process.

After the meal the pastor, with members of the pilot group, makes a brief presentation about the Covenant Discipleship group. This presentation should include brief explanations of the General Rule of Discipleship, the group covenant, and the group meeting. Conclude with a concise description of the office of class leader as one outcome of Covenant Discipleship groups and an essential piece of the congregation's disciple-making mission. Explain that the goal of the weekend event is to form new Covenant Discipleship groups. Members of the pilot group will join the new groups. At the end of the after-dinner presentation, invite people who want to learn more to return to the church on Saturday morning when a three-hour seminar will be presented. The workshop will go into more detail about the Covenant Discipleship process and conclude with a brief role play of a group meeting.

The Saturday Morning Seminar and Role Play

On Saturday morning the pastor and pilot group members lead a three-hour seminar on Covenant Discipleship with members of the congregation. Topics for discussion include the following:

- The General Rule of Discipleship
- The covenant
- Covenant writing
- The Covenant Discipleship group dynamics
- Role play of a Covenant Discipleship group meeting
- Questions and discussion

Hold the seminar in a room in which participants can be seated at tables; round tables work best. Provide coffee, tea, juice, water, and light snacks for participants. PowerPoint slides for this presentation may be downloaded from the Discipleship Ministries website: http:// umcdiscipleship.org/covenantdiscipleship.

Allow thirty minutes for a covenant-writing exercise. Use the sample preambles, clauses, and conclusions included in the appendix of this book as aids for covenant writing. This will give participants a hands-on experience of covenant writing. It will help them grasp the importance of the covenant to the group process.

Conclude the seminar with the pilot group leading a ten-minute role play of a group meeting. This is an essential part of the seminar, as it gives participants a glimpse of the dynamic of the group meeting. It helps people see the nature of accountability as simply showing up to give an account of what has been done, or not done, in relation to the group covenant. They need to see that accountability is not focused on evaluation, judgment, guilt, or shame. The role play illuminates the way group members care for and support one another, aiming to help one another become more faithful, dependable follow-ers of Jesus Christ and leaders in discipleship for the congregation.

The role play also reveals the pastor as being a fellow member of the group. The pastor should not lead the role play. It is important the pastor is present as a fellow disciple of Jesus Christ giving his or her account just like everyone else.

Allow time after the role play for questions and discussion. This is a time for the pilot group members, including the pastor, to answer questions and discuss concerns raised by participants and potential members of new groups.

Sunday Worship

The Sunday morning worship service is the climax of the pilot year and Covenant Discipleship Weekend. The baptismal covenant and discipleship in the Wesleyan tradition are the focus of the service. This service is typically planned to coincide with the Baptism of the Lord Sunday (First Sunday after the Epiphany). Plan for a service of Word *and* Table. It is most appropriate to include the congregational reaffirmation of the baptismal covenant.[4] You will find a suggested order of worship at the Discipleship Ministries website: http://umc-discipleship.org/covenantdiscipleship.

Make and distribute to everyone in the congregation a Covenant Discipleship response card. Include on the card the General Rule of Discipleship and a brief description of the Covenant Discipleship group, followed by a list of three possible responses:

- I want to join a new Covenant Discipleship group.
  List the days and times you are available to meet for one-hour each week. Please provide your e-mail address and telephone number.
- I am interested in joining a Covenant Discipleship group in the future. Now is not a good time for me.
- I do not want to join a Covenant Discipleship group. I will pray for the groups and the disciple-making mission of this congregation.

Distribute the response cards to the entire congregation through the mail or e-mail or both. Instruct members who desire to join a Covenant Discipleship group but cannot be present for the Covenant Sunday to return the cards by mail or via an e-mail reply. Instruct members to bring their completed cards with them to the Covenant Sunday worship service. Also distribute cards with the order of worship.

Invite the congregation to leave completed response cards at the front of the church when they come forward to reaffirm the baptismal covenant or receive the sacrament at the Lord's table. Or instruct the congregation to place their completed cards in the offering plates as they are passed during the offering.

The pastor and members of the pilot group receive and compile the response cards following the worship service. Sort through all the response cards. Record them in a spreadsheet for each of the three possible responses. A reply should be sent to each person who returned a card. Thank respondents for taking the time to reply. Invite those who indicate the desire to join a group to a meeting with members of the pilot group.

Follow-Up Book Study

I recommend that the congregation purchase a supply of this book to be distributed to members who intend to join a Covenant Discipleship group. The cost of the books could be recovered by inviting the people to purchase them from the church. Orient new group members to the Covenant Discipleship group process with a four-week study of this book. Focus the study on the chapters focusing on the General Rule of Discipleship and Covenant Discipleship groups. Also familiarize them with the chapter on class leaders. This will help those persons whom God calls to the office of class leader to be open and to respond when the time is right.

At the final session of the book study, determine the days and times of the new Covenant Discipleship group meetings. Assign a pilot group member to each of the new groups. Ideally, the pilot group members will remain with the new groups. They bring their experience with them into the group, acting like the sourdough starter added to a loaf of bread dough. The sourdough transforms the regular bread dough into sourdough. The pilot group member brings experience with weekly accountability for living the Christian life in relation to the group's covenant, which is shaped by the General Rule of Discipleship.

In the event pilot group members refuse to leave their first group to join a new group, they must agree to meet with both groups through the new group's covenant-writing process. The pilot group members guide the new groups through the work of writing their covenant. Once the covenant is written and signed, the pilot group member leads the group through three meetings, facilitating and modeling the process of giving an account for each covenant clause. Once that process is complete and the new group is comfortable meeting on its own, the pilot group member withdraws and meets only with his or her original group, but continues to be available to the new group when questions or concerns arise.

Supporting Covenant Discipleship

After the pilot year, when the congregation has two or more groups meeting every week, it will need a means to support the groups and ensure that they keep to their mission of forming leaders in discipleship through weekly accountability and support for living the Christian life.

Conveners and the Convener Council

The best way to provide the essential support for this ministry is by creating a convener council led by the pastor. Each Covenant Discipleship group selects one member to serve as its convener. A convener is a member of the Covenant Discipleship group who serves on the convener council as liaison between the group and the pastor. The council consists of the conveners for each of the Covenant Discipleship groups and the pastor. The council meets quarterly. The agenda of the meeting is for each of the conveners to report to the council how their group is functioning. The reporting is done with care so as to avoid breaking the confidence of the respective groups. This process is akin to taking the temperature of each group. If the group is functioning smoothly, then there is not much to report. The council meeting is an opportunity to bring questions, challenges, and concerns a group may be experiencing to a group of people who can help keep the groups on track. The convener council is also a way for the pastor to keep apprised of the health of the various groups. The council plays a critical role in supporting the Covenant Discipleship ministry and keeping the groups focused on the mission of forming leaders in discipleship who help the congregation with its disciple-making mission.

Another way the convener council supports and sustains Covenant Discipleship is for the council to have a representative sit on the church council. Having one of the conveners, along with the pastor, participate in the church council will go a long way to ensure that the ministry is integral to the congregation's missional life. This person may be elected by the congregation.

The role of convener is an important role that is ideally shared. If possible, a convener serves in that role for one year. Members take turns serving as conveners. No one person should be expected to serve indefinitely. Just as leadership of the weekly meeting rotates among group members from week to week, each member takes a turn serving as convener for a year.

The Pastor's Participation

The pastor is critical to the success of Covenant Discipleship in the congregation. The pastor *must* be an active participant in the pilot Covenant Discipleship group. Why should pastors participate in a Covenant Discipleship group with members of the congregation they are appointed to serve? I can think of at least two reasons: pastors are disciples too, and pastors learn about discipleship from disciples.

Pastors Are Disciples Too

Pastoral leadership is filled with demands and expectations that often crowd out practices that nurture holiness of heart and life. When I ask a pastor about his or her prayer life, I too often hear them say, "I don't have time to pray." They tell me that planning and leading worship is a job that prevents them from worshiping God with the congregation on Sunday morning. Scripture reading is limited to sermon preparation. Their time is consumed by the demands and expectations of the congregation: committee meetings, sermon preparation, and visiting members who are homebound, in nursing homes, and in the hospital.

Pastors are frequently under pressure to meet the demands of church members and conference leadership. Their time is focused on serving the church, district, and conference. The demands of pastoral ministry frequently do not include intentional time for attending to the pastor's discipleship. I recall a meeting with the pastor-parish relations committee of a congregation I once served. The committee was preparing for my departure. The purpose of the meeting was to put together a profile of a pastor who would be a good fit for the congregation. I led them in a brainstorming session in which we wrote on newsprint the characteristics and skills members of the committee felt were most needed: biblical preacher, good singer and worship leader, good with youth and children, likes to visit members who are homebound and in nursing homes, good teacher, married with children, and so on. After they had completed their list, I noticed there was no mention of prayer. I asked the committee if they wanted a pastor who was a person who prayed regularly. After an uncomfortable silence, the chairman said, "Yeah. That'd be good. As long as he did it on his own time."

I suspect this is a typical congregation. Prayer and spiritual disciplines are not regarded as essential to faithful pastoral ministry. Members have been trained to expect their pastors to cater to their personal needs and expectations. Spiritual disciplines and discipleship are seen as a worthy hobby but not integral to pastoral leadership.

While many conferences are recognizing that pastors need time and space to attend to their own discipleship, the culture of the congregation typically does not.

One way to address this need is for pastors to be in a Covenant Discipleship group with laity from the congregation(s) they are appointed to serve. The weekly process of mutual accountability and support for the practice of discipleship, which is shaped by the General Rule of Discipleship, provides the structure pastors need to be intentional about attending to their own relationship with God. It also helps congregation members see that their pastor is a disciple of Jesus Christ just like them. He or she does not have all the answers. The pastor, just like everyone else, needs the help and support of fellow Christians.

When pastors participate in a Covenant Discipleship group with laity, the congregation sees that discipleship is relational. Theological training and ordination do not exempt anyone from their need for fellow Christians to help them live as faithful witnesses to Jesus Christ in the world. While laywomen and men in the pastor's group help him grow in holiness of heart and life, other church members may be encouraged to be more intentional about their discipleship. If their pastor is intentional about his discipleship, perhaps others in the congregation will imitate him.

Pastors Learn about Discipleship from Disciples

Most pastors live in a church bubble. Most of the people they encounter on any given day are church members, other clergy, or conference staff. Most meetings they attend are with other church people, whether of their own or another denomination. The typical pastor's days are consumed by the church and church-related people. Therefore, their experience of discipleship is limited by their vocation.

Pastors need to be in Covenant Discipleship groups with laity because the men and women in the group will teach them about discipleship. Christians live and work in the world in ways most clergy can only imagine. Laywomen and men encounter people, situations, and choices most clergy never will. The truth of discipleship comes into sharper focus for the pastor when he or she listen to the stories laymen and women tell week after week as they account for how they strive to be faithful to Christ in the workplace, on the street, or in the fields, guided by the group's covenant.

When pastors participate in Covenant Discipleship groups, they receive the support and accountability they need to grow in holiness of heart and life. They also learn about discipleship as they listen to their fellow group members share stories of how they witness to Jesus Christ in the office, factory, shop, school, on the streets, and in the fields. When the congregation knows their pastor is working on her discipleship every week in a group of fellow Christians, they learn that she is a follower of Jesus Christ just like they are. If their pastor acknowledges she needs the help of other Christians to grow as a disciple, then they too can do the same. As a result, pursuing holiness of heart and life makes its way into the culture of the congregation's life and work.

An Ongoing Process

After Covenant Discipleship groups are established and recognized as an important, foundational part of the congregation's disciple-making mission, the Covenant Discipleship Weekend becomes an annual event in the congregation's life. The responsibility for planning and implementing the weekend is part of the convener council's work, with cooperation and support from the church council and others.

The hope and expectation is that after two or more years some of the Covenant Discipleship group members will respond to the call to serve in the office of class leader. The annual Covenant Discipleship Sunday should include the commissioning of class leaders and acknowledgment of each Covenant Discipleship group. Each group could present its covenant as an offering to the congregation. The service could conclude with a consecration of the Covenant Discipleship groups, the class leaders, and class members.

Conclusion

The foundation of a house is important to its structural integrity. Foundation problems are typically found after damage to the walls and ceilings becomes visible. Laying the foundation on solid ground or bedrock is essential to the long-term soundness of the house.

Covenant Discipleship connects the foundation of the congregation's disciple-making mission to the bedrock of Jesus' teachings. It equips Christians to act on his teachings through mutual accountability and support. Covenant Discipleship shapes holy habits that ensure the congregation is a Christ-centered community with people who hear Jesus' words and act upon them. It is a proven means of forming leaders in discipleship who "have the mind which was in Christ, and walk just as he walked."[5]

Covenant Discipleship groups require pastoral participation and support through the convener council. The congregation supports the ministry by electing one of the conveners to serve on the church council. The pastor- (or staff-) parish relations committee (PPRC) supports the ministry by encouraging and expecting the pastor to participate in a Covenant Discipleship group. At the time of a change of pastoral appointment the committee encourages the cabinet and bishop to appoint a pastor who will support, encourage, and participate in Covenant Discipleship. When a pastoral candidate is introduced to the PPRC, they tell him or her about the importance of Covenant Discipleship groups and class leaders to the mission of the congregation and inquire about the candidate's experience with the ministry. If the candidate does not have previous experience with Covenant Discipleship, the PPRC will inform him or her of the resources available from Discipleship Ministries and contact the director of Wesleyan Leadership, who can provide necessary training.

The most important contribution of covenant discipleship groups is the extent to which they provide leadership in discipleship for congregations. Individual members are, of course, helped personally by their weekly meetings. But the true purpose and function of the groups is to exemplify methodical, reliable discipleship. By holding themselves accountable for witnessing to Christ and for living out his teachings in the world, they can help to form faithful Christian disciples, and help congregations to be more vital in ministry and mission.

If covenant discipleship groups are to provide this leadership, they must be allowed to assume their proper role in the life and work of congregations. Their insight will often be unexpected, sometimes critical, but almost always a source of spiritual discernment on boards and committees, in Sunday school classes, in youth groups, and in the church's ministries of compassion, justice, worship, and devotion. They will not necessarily occupy traditional positions of leadership, but their influence will be substantial— if, that is, they are acknowledged as leaders in discipleship, and if their groups are carefully formed and nurtured.

—David Lowes Watson
Forming Christian Disciples, p. 113

CHAPTER 6

Class Leaders for Today: Disciple-Making Disciples

> The gifts he gave were that some would be apostles, some prophets, some evangelists, some pastors and teachers, to equip the saints for the work of ministry, for building up the body of Christ, until all of us come to the unity of the faith and of the knowledge of the Son of God, to maturity, to the measure of the full stature of Christ. We must no longer be children, tossed to and fro and blown about by every wind of doctrine, by people's trickery, by their craftiness in deceitful scheming. But speaking the truth in love, we must grow up in every way into him who is the head, into Christ, from whom the whole body, joined and knit together by every ligament with which it is equipped, as each part is working properly, promotes the body's growth in building itself up in love.
>
> —Ephesians 4:11-16

Remember the image of the Gothic cathedral in chapter 3? Recall the importance of the pillars that support the church, allowing it to perform its mission to glorify God and help people experience God's goodness, majesty, and mystery. The pillars allow for the large windows with multicolored stained glass that fill the church with light. They create a home with a table at the center, where people come to be forgiven, fed, and equipped to join Christ's mission in the world.

In Ephesians 4:11 the apostle Paul describes the fivefold ministry of apostles, prophets, evangelists, pastors, and teachers who God has placed in every congregation. They are like the pillars that support the Gothic cathedral. Their obedience to Jesus' teachings keeps the church grounded in his life and mission. These leaders in discipleship ensure that the church is centered in Christ as a sign-community for the reign of God. When the church strives to keep the promises of the baptismal covenant, it allows grace to flow freely. When grace flows, the Holy Spirit is free to work, and people are more likely to cooperate and develop the gifts God has given them for "building up the body of Christ" (Eph. 4:11-12).

In the Wesleyan Methodist tradition, many of the people Paul identifies as having the gift to be apostles, prophets, evangelists, pastor, and teachers have served in the office of class leader. For many years, class leaders served as shepherds and teachers in Methodist congregations. They were role models, mentors, and coaches in discipleship. Their witness enabled congregations to faithfully carry out the mission of making disciples of Jesus Christ who join in his world-transforming mission.

The class meeting was the place where men and women were formed, equipped, and supported in their ministry as class leaders. Today Covenant Discipleship groups form the class leaders the church needs to faithfully carry out its mission in the world.

Class Leaders: Pillars of the Church

The title *class leader* is troublesome. When people hear the term, they usually assume it describes a Sunday school teacher. Others associate it with leaders of social class. This confusion occurs because most United Methodists have no memory of class leaders serving in their church. The office was neglected and ignored for decades before the requirement was removed from the *Book of Discipline* in the early twentieth century. Class leaders and class meetings were once essential to Methodist identity and mission, but are now forgotten and neglected.

It is important for us to understand that class leaders and class meetings were the sinews of Methodism.[1] John Wesley provided the class leader's job description in the General Rules:

> That it may the more easily be discerned whether they are indeed working out their own salvation, each society is divided into smaller companies, called classes, according to their respective places of abode. There are about twelve persons in a class, one of whom is styled the leader. It is his duty:
>
> 1. To see each person in his class once a week at least, in order: to inquire how their souls prosper; to advise, reprove, comfort or exhort, as occasion may require; to receive what they are willing to give toward the relief of the preachers, church, and poor.
>
> 2. To meet the ministers and the stewards of the society once a week, in order: to inform the minister of any that are sick, or of any that walk disorderly and will not be reproved; to pay the stewards what they have received of their several classes in the week preceding.[2]

The function of the class leader was similar to a coach. Class leaders taught people in their classes the basic practices and beliefs of Christian discipleship. They also provided the support and accountability people needed to apply what they learned to their daily lives. Class leaders provided frontline pastoral care within the early Methodist societies in Great Britain and North America.

Disciples Make Disciples

Class leaders as defined in the Methodist tradition are the leaders in discipleship every congregation needs. They are called by God and equipped to help the congregation cooperate with the Holy Spirit working to form others into faithful, dependable disciples of Jesus Christ. A seminary education is not a prerequisite for the work of making disciples. All that is required is "faith working through love" (Gal. 5:6).

Class leaders are laywomen and laymen from all walks of life who remember their baptism and center their lives upon Jesus Christ and his mission. They renounce the spiritual forces of wickedness; reject the evil powers of this world and repent of their sins; accept the freedom and power God gives to resist evil, injustice, and oppression in whatever forms they present themselves; and confess Jesus Christ as Savior, placing their whole trust in his grace, and promise to serve him as Lord, in union with the church.[3]

Class leaders are members of the congregation who hear Jesus' words and act on them (Matt. 7:24ff). They partner with the pastor, other leaders, and the Holy Spirit to ensure that the congregation keeps the promise made in the baptismal commendation to "do all in your power to increase their faith, confirm their hope, and perfect them in love."[4]

The following stanzas from Charles Wesley's hymn "Try Us, O God, and Search the Ground" beautifully summarize the Wesleyan way of making disciples and living the Christian life. It is a deeply relational effort initiated by God the Father, accompanied by God the Son, and empowered by God the Holy Spirit. We see in these lines that we do not make ourselves disciples of Jesus Christ by our own faith and strength of will. Rather, Christ, who promises to accompany us in the relationships with seasoned disciples he brings into our life, calls each of us into discipleship and accompanies us along the way to holiness of heart and life.

> Try us, O God, and search the ground
> Of every sinful heart!
> Whate'er of sin in us is found,
> O bid it all depart!
>
> When to the right or left we stray,
> Leave us not comfortless,

But guide our feet into the way
Of everlasting peace.

Help us to help each other, Lord,
Each other's cross to bear;
Let all their friendly aid afford,
And feel each other's care.

Help us to build each other up,
Our little stock improve;
Increase our faith, confirm our hope,
And perfect us in love.[5]

Class Leaders Today

Today, class leaders are women and men who meet weekly with their Covenant Discipleship group. After consultation and discernment with the pastor and the committee on nominations and leader development, they are commissioned by the congregation to serve as a class leader.[6]

Class leaders are given missional responsibility for up to twenty members of the congregation. This means class leaders help members of their "class" live the Christian life shaped by the General Rule of Discipleship: "To witness to Jesus Christ in the world and to follow his teachings through acts of compassion, justice, worship, and devotion under the guidance of the Holy Spirit."[7] Class leaders work as partners with the pastor to lead the congregation in making disciples of Jesus Christ who are equipped to join his mission in the world.

Class leaders meet monthly with the pastor. These meetings give the pastor an opportunity to support and train class leaders. Class leaders, in turn, help the pastor monitor the pulse of the congregation and more effectively lead, because he or she is regularly updated on the spiritual well-being of members who are in regular contact with a class leader.

Why Class Leaders?

The mission of The United Methodist Church is to make disciples of Jesus Christ for the transformation of the world. Scripture tells us that disciple making is a relational process. Discipleship is the way of life of a person who knows, follows, and orders his or her life according to the teachings of Jesus Christ. We know from the Gospels that Jesus had twelve male disciples whom the Gospel writers identified by name. There were also women: the sisters Mary and Martha, Mary Magdalene, along with others. I think we can safely say that Jesus himself discipled fifteen to twenty people.

How then can we reasonably expect any pastor of a congregation today to do any better than Jesus? How can anyone expect a pastor to make disciples of more than fifteen to twenty people in any congregation or charge? The genius of the system of class meetings and class leaders developed by John and Charles Wesley is that it is a disciple-making partnership between the appointed leaders (clergy) and the leaders in discipleship God has placed in each congregation. The system assumes that God calls men and women to the ministry of missional leadership with their peers in each congregation of his church. These leaders partner with the appointed pastor to make disciples of Jesus Christ who join in his mission in the world.

Jesus discipled fifteen to twenty people. He equipped them to disciple others. They became apostles who discipled fifteen to twenty others. When we do the math, we quickly see how the Jesus movement multiplied and grew.

The Wesleyan "method" retraditioned Jesus' way of disciple making. It is built upon relationships centered in Jesus Christ and equipping people to join his mission in the world. Pastors are free to devote themselves to the work they are called and ordained to do: proclaim the gospel, administer the sacraments, lead in serving with the poor in the world, and ordering the life of the congregation. They work as partners with people God has called to the disciple-making mission of equipping people to join in Christ's mission in the world.

Covenant Discipleship groups develop the leaders needed to retradition the class meeting for today. The system of class leaders and classes discussed in this chapter is based in scripture and the Wesleyan tradition of disciple making and mission. It helps congregations keep the promises made in the baptismal covenant and provides Christians the means to live and witness as faithful disciples of Jesus Christ.

Tradition and Sustaining Faithful Witnesses

Tradition is the act of handing down a custom from one generation to the next. For Christians, tradition is how the gospel *of* Jesus and the gospel *about* Jesus are handed down from one generation to another. Too often tradition is equated with the trappings and practices of an institution. Tradition is sometimes used by people seeking to resist change by clinging to practices, beliefs, and places long past. Tradition, when properly understood and practiced, is how the church remains centered in Christ "to serve the present age" in language, symbols, and practices they understand.[8]

Jesus summarizes his gospel in Mark 1:15 saying, "The time is fulfilled, and the kingdom of God has come near; repent, and believe in the good news." Jesus came into the world to proclaim God's kingdom. He lived and preached the message of God's rule of love, righteousness, and justice breaking into the world. God's shalom is a present reality and a promised hope. Jesus describes his mission in Luke 4:18-19. The Sermon on the Mount (Matt. 5–7) gives his followers a glimpse of life in the reign of God. The great commandments (Matt. 22:34-40; Mark 12:28-34; and Luke 10:25-28) are Jesus' summary of how we are to live as citizens of God's kingdom.

Related to the gospel *of* Jesus Christ is the gospel *about* Jesus Christ, summarized in Acts 10:34-43. Jesus is the incarnation of God's love for the world (John 3:16). Sins are forgiven. Relationship with God, neighbors, and self are restored. In Jesus, God provides the grace required to realize God's acceptance and live as children of God's household (2 Cor. 5:16-21).

Tradition entails practices and teaching that enable the church to build and sustain a community that faithfully witnesses to Jesus Christ in the world. Over the course of several years of pastoral experience, John and Charles Wesley established several traditions among the people called Methodists. These traditions helped sustain the Methodists, who were both missional and evangelical. The primary purpose of these traditions was to keep the Methodist societies centered on Jesus Christ, his teachings, and his mission.

Class leaders and class meetings were the strength of the Methodist movement. They were incubators of discipleship that formed countless women and men as witnesses of Jesus Christ in the world. The goal of Covenant Discipleship groups is to retradition the class meeting and class leaders for The United Methodist Church today.

Retraditioning the Office of Class Leader

Retraditioning means contextualizing a practice that worked in the past so that it works and bears fruit in the present. The class leaders and classes this book advocates and supports are adapted from the early Methodist model developed by John and Charles Wesley. The class meeting practiced in the Methodist Episcopal Church of the nineteenth century will not work today. The work David Lowes Watson did beginning in the mid-1980s sought to adapt the essential elements of the early class meeting to the culture and needs of the contemporary church.

Watson's years of research and writing about the eighteenth-century Methodist class meeting led him to the conclusion that these important, long disused, Methodist traditions could be retraditioned by the contemporary church to become a powerful means of grace and Christian formation for today.

Watson realized that the congregation that wanted to retradition the class meeting must first develop members to serve as class leaders. Covenant Discipleship groups and the General Rule of Discipleship were developed to meet the need of leader formation. Weekly accountability and support for living the Christian life shapes and prepares members to answer God's call to the office of class leader.

It typically takes two years for Covenant Discipleship groups to take root in a congregation. The first year is the pilot year that is spent learning how the groups work, interpreting the General Rule of Discipleship, and the work of the groups to the congregation. At the beginning of the second year the groups are opened to everyone in the congregation. Participation increases as more people get involved in the Covenant Discipleship groups.

During the introductory two years, the pastor and group members need to keep the General Rule of Discipleship in front of the congregation. They encourage the church council to adopt it as the congregation's rule of life that shapes its ministry and mission.[9] By the end of the second year, members of the congregation should be able to recite the General Rule by heart.

The introductory years are also time to prepare the congregation for class leaders and classes. The pastor and pilot group members familiarize the church council, staff/pastor-parish relations committee, and other key leaders with the office of class leader and classes as missional groupings within the congregation. They encourage them to be role models when the office of class leader is introduced and to help congregation members look forward to and welcome having a relationship with a class leader as their discipleship coach.

The Class Today

The class is an effective way to extend the General Rule of Discipleship into the congregation, beyond Covenant Discipleship groups. A class is a grouping of fifteen to twenty members of the congregation. "These classes are not the same as Sunday school classes, nor are they convened as class meetings."[10] Members agree to have a class leader relate to them as their discipleship coach. Class membership may be determined using various criteria: neighborhood or zip code, length of church membership, and so on. "Each class should be broadly representative of the congregation as a whole. The last thing a class should be is a grouping of 'problem' members, or 'inactives,' or those with special needs."[11]

The class is a missional grouping bound together by class members' relationship with a class leader. The class leader's responsibility is to regularly contact each member of his or her class in order to nurture and encourage them in their discipleship, shaped by the General Rule of Discipleship. Their conversation has a clear purpose: "To provide the class members with help and encouragement in the basics of their discipleship. As the relationship develops, the class leader will become a trusted friend. But the friendship will be a firm one, because it will always be directed toward an accountability for faithful discipleship."[12]

I refer to the classes as "missional groupings" because their purpose is the mission of the congregation: to make disciples of Jesus Christ for the transformation of the world. Class leaders provide the friendship, support, and accountability the congregation promises to provide at each baptism to help professing members live their baptismal covenant. They watch over members of their classes in love, they pray for them, and they walk with them, helping them to grow in holiness of heart and life. Class leaders serve as discipleship coaches, teaching and reminding the class members to practice the basics of discipleship. As they practice their discipleship, shaped by the General Rule of Discipleship, members are formed as disciples of Jesus Christ.

Why No Class Meeting?

The first step toward what became the original class meetings of John Wesley's time was to have class leaders visit fifteen to twenty members of the society, house to house. The premise for the weekly visits was to retire the mortgage on the first Methodist meetinghouse by collecting a penny from members. When the leaders visited each class member to collect the weekly penny, they also listened to the member talk about how their week had gone. Before leaving the home, the two Methodists prayed together. The leaders met with John Wesley at the end of the month to give him the pennies they collected and to give a report on the general spiritual well-being of society members. They eventually decided to change the process and require the Methodists to meet weekly as a group with their class leader.

Because The United Methodist Church today harbors no memory of the weekly class meeting or class leaders, trying to impose such a scheme is impractical and premature.

> We must remember that the early class meetings were groups of men and women whose disciplined commitment was far from that of the average church member of today. They agreed to abide by a very specific set of rules. They submitted to a quarterly examination in order to keep their membership in good standing. They attended their weekly class meetings, not only as a means of grace but also as a condition of membership. They were "little churches" within the church, and not at all representative of the rank and file parishioners of the eighteenth century Church of England.
>
> To the extent that The United Methodist Church is the equivalent of the Church of England in Wesley's day, we cannot expect this disciplined lifestyle from the average church member. But we can, indeed we should, expect it from the leaders of the church, both clergy and laity. This has been the purpose of traditioning the early class meeting as covenant discipleship groups for the church of today—a means of leadership development. Perhaps by grace, we shall have a similar accountability across the entire church. But first, we must establish leaders in discipleship who can begin to extend the General Rule of Discipleship to *missional* groupings of church members. These discipleship classes may become class meetings; but only when they are ready.[13]

The Class Leader as Discipleship Coach

I once read an interview in *Sports Illustrated* magazine with a producer for Fox Sports. She worked on the broadcasts for Major

League Baseball games. One of her jobs was to listen to the recorded conversations on the field between players, coaches, managers, and umpires. If you watch MLB games you know that select players, coaches, umpires, and managers are equipped with small microphones during the game. During breaks in the action the network will occasionally broadcast a snippet of a conversation between the player and the first-base coach or between the catcher and home-plate umpire. As a baseball fan, I find these conversations to usually be quite interesting. The interviewer asked the producer, "In all the on-field chatter you've listened to over the years, what surprised you the most?" She answered, "I was really surprised by how frequently the coaches reminded their players to pay attention to the fundamentals of the game. Things like, keeping track of how many outs there are in the inning, watch for the third-base coach as you round second, or make sure you touch all the bases, simple, basic things every little leaguer knows."

She is talking about grown men who are professional baseball players. They have played the game their whole lives and are playing in the Major Leagues. This means they are the best in the world at playing baseball. In spite of all those years of practice and experience, their coaches know their players need to be reminded, over and over again, to pay attention to the basics, to the fundamentals of the game.

The coaches she is talking about are the men responsible for helping players improve and master the basic skills needed to play baseball to the best of their ability: hitting, throwing, running, catching, and thinking. The coaches were also players when they were younger. Their playing experience enables them to connect with the players and get the very best out of them. They share their experience and wisdom gained from years of playing in the minor and major leagues. The goal of coaching is to improve the player's skills to get the best possible performance from them over and over again. Along the way to excellence, the coach also contributes to the formation of the player as an honorable human being.

A mark of a good coach is the ability to listen and understand the players. He learns the player's story, where they come from, who their families are, who and what they love, what motivates them. This ability to learn the person helps the player trust the coach. The coach wants the player to trust that he is with him, he is someone the player can trust.

Class leaders are seasoned disciples of Jesus Christ. They meet weekly with a Covenant Discipleship group. The group provides the accountability and support the class leader needs to live as a witness to Jesus Christ in the world. He or she has experience with discipleship. The discipline of weekly accountability equips the class leader to perceive and respond to God's call to be a discipleship coach for the church.

Class leaders remind class members to practice the basics of discipleship, shaped by the General Rule of Discipleship. Like a coach, she listens to and learns each member's story, his strengths and weaknesses. In particular, the class leader discerns the spiritual gifts of each class member and helps him or her use and develop that gift through disciplined practice of the basics of discipleship. The class leader knows that practicing the basics, as described in the General Rule of Discipleship, opens the class member to the Holy Spirit, who will lead and develop his or her gifts in ways that contribute to Christ's mission in the church and the world. The class leader's job is to keep the class members centered in Christ and his mission in their lives and in the world.

Getting to Know the Class

Class leaders serve as partners with the pastor. The ministry of class leaders is important, because the work of Christian formation cannot be the sole responsibility of the appointed pastor. In fact, for most of the history of the church, laywomen and men have served as disciples who disciple others. They are better suited than clergy for the work of disciple making, because their lives are not consumed by the church and its "business."

Pastors are responsible for preaching the gospel, administering the sacraments, and ordering the life of the congregation. The laity, class leaders in particular, are to love and care for one another and do all in their power to increase faith, confirm hope in Christ, and perfect one another in love. This is affirmed in the baptismal covenant with these words: "With God's help we will proclaim the good news and live according to the example of Christ. We will surround these persons with a community of love and forgiveness, that they may grow in their trust of God, and be found faithful in their service to others. We will pray for them, that they may be true disciples who walk in the way that leads to life."[14] When the congregation strives to live out the promises made in the baptismal covenant, it is more likely to become a community in which everyone is known by name. More than knowing everyone by name, members are provided the help and resources needed to be "true disciples who walk in the way that leads to life."[15] This requires leaders who acknowledge the diversity of faith and experience present in every congregation.

As they begin their work, it is important for class leaders to understand they are *not* pastoral counselors. They are discipleship coaches. Their task is to walk alongside members of their class and help each one grow in holiness of heart and life (loving God and loving those whom God loves), shaped by the General Rule of Discipleship. Their goal is to form relationships of mutual trust that allow them to help each class member grow in his or her practice of the basics of discipleship (acts of compassion, justice, worship, and devotion).

The Introductory Meeting

The first step is to send a letter of introduction to each member of the class.

> Point out in the letter that you are available primarily to help them with their discipleship, and to be a source of information about the life and work of the congregation. Let them know that they can expect you to visit them personally in the near future, when you will explain the nature and purpose

of your office more fully, and ask them to confirm that they wish to be in your class.

As you schedule these visits, or perhaps while you are making them, there may be people on the list who do not wish to be in your class. Since the names were agreed by the leaders' meeting, including the pastor, this is not likely to happen very often. But when it does, you may be disappointed, and perhaps a little hurt. Report any such refusals to the leaders' meeting, and ask for the reaction of your colleagues. You will probably find that every class leader has had similar refusals; in these early days of recovering the office of class leader, this is bound to happen. The important thing is that no one should feel pressured into accepting your leadership. The idea will take time to grow in each congregation. But it will gain acceptance, as will you and your fellow class leaders. The person who refuses to join your class this year may well ask to join next year.[16]

Make appointments to meet each member of the class. These are face-to-face meetings, preferably in the home. The initial meeting place must provide for a private, uninterrupted conversation between the class leader and class member. If an entire family is assigned, then it must be a time when everyone can be present. Allow forty-five to fifty minutes focused on the following agenda:

1. Explanation of the office of class leader
2. Personal introductions
3. Explanation of the General Rule of Discipleship
4. Response and discussion

At the conclusion of the meeting tell the person that you will contact the member in about a month to inquire about parts of the General Rule of Discipleship for which the member would like your help.

Before you leave offer a brief prayer inviting the Holy Spirit to guide them toward a relationship of mutual trust, care, and love for Christ, his church, the world, and one another as they embark on this new adventure in discipleship. Invite class members to offer a prayer.

The initial round of meetings is an intense time for the class leader. Allow plenty of time between visits. Do not schedule more than two meetings in any given day. This will be a challenging and rewarding time that will help you gain confidence in your role and responsibility as a class leader.

What Not to Do with a Class

As the class leader begins living into relationships with various class members, the leader needs to be mindful of what to avoid doing with them:

1. *Do not overload members.* Members of the class will have a diversity of experience with discipleship. Some may be in a Covenant Discipleship group like you. For most, the notion of Christian discipline will be a new, even foreign, concept. Tread lightly. Resist the temptation to give advice and suggestions for various areas of the General Rule of Discipleship.

Listen. Ask open-ended questions. Take time to understand each person's ideas, beliefs, and needs related to faith and discipleship. Meet each person where he or she is. Let members know you are committed to walking with them as they learn and live as a disciple of Jesus Christ.

2. *Do not talk about other class members.* The only information to be shared with other members of the class are their names and contact information. Your task with each member is to build a relationship of trust between you and him or her. In your interactions and conversation, focus on their discipleship. Do not talk about what other class members are doing, no matter how innocuous. If each person is confident you will not talk about what he or she is doing with other class members, then members are more likely to trust you as their class leader.

Remember, at this stage, the class is a missional group within the congregation. It is not a small group. Your focus is on the one-with-one relationships you have with each member. "Whatever may happen with other small groups in the congregation, and whatever is being done with class meetings in other Methodist traditions, the only common denominator of your class at this stage is you, the class leader. They will accept this relationship with you far more readily than with a group."[17]

3. *Do not attempt to convene the class.* "Your members have not been asked to attend class meetings. They have rather been asked to accept you as their class leader. This is not to say that your class should never get together. Someone may suggest a discussion on an issue of common concern in their discipleship, or to work together on a particular service project. There may even be the desire to have a social evening. But it will be important for these suggestions to surface spontaneously from the members themselves, rather than from you. There are already plenty of church meetings for everyone to attend; and if you initiate yet another meeting, you will have the burden of organizing it and making it worthwhile. If your class does indicate a desire to get together, let the members make the suggestion, not you."[18]

Continuing Contact with Class Members

The class leader can take a number of positive actions to build relationships with class members.

1. *Model discipleship.* In your role as class leader members will look to you and the way you conduct yourself in the congregation. One of the most effective ways you can lead members of your class in their discipleship is to live as a faithful disciple of Jesus Christ yourself. Be faithful in attendance in your Covenant Discipleship group. Group members will provide the support and accountability you need in your pursuit of holiness of heart and life and in your ministry as class leader.

2. *Inform class members about the congregation's ministries.* Keep class members informed about the congregation's ministries. Relate the various ministries and programs to the areas of the General Rule of Discipleship: acts of compassion, acts of justice, acts of

worship, and acts of devotion. Highlight opportunities the congregation offers that fit each of these areas of discipleship and encourage
them to participate as they are able.

3. *Meet with class members.* At a minimum, meet face to face
with each class member once a quarter to check in with them about
their discipleship in relation to the General Rule of Discipleship. Most
meetings will be informal and arranged spontaneously. You may be
invited to have lunch after worship on Sunday afternoon or to meet
at a coffee shop during the week. You may run into a member by
chance on the street, at the grocery store, at a ball game, or anywhere
in public. These are all opportunities to build the relationship and to
ask class members about how they're doing with their discipleship.

Electronic and social media are valuable means of keeping in
touch with class members. Send weekly text messages with words of
encouragement to each member. Create a "secret" Facebook group
for class members. Secret groups are visible to only the persons who
are invited to join. This is a way for you to provide reminders about
opportunities in the congregation and in the community to practice acts of compassion, justice, worship, or devotion. Post articles
you find helpful or pieces you think would help one or more class
members.

In all you do, be mindful to keep Christ at the center. Remember
your role is to help members of your class with their discipleship. You
are their discipleship coach, the one who cares for them enough to
gently remind them to practice the basics of discipleship, shaped by
the General Rule of Discipleship. You are their friend. But the friendship is centered in your shared relationship with Jesus Christ and
the baptismal covenant. The aim of the relationship is to help each
member learn the meaning and practice of living as a Christian who
"professes to pursue holiness of heart and life."[19]

Discerning the Call to Be a Class Leader

I will never forget a telephone call I received from a woman serving as a licensed local pastor in rural Iowa. She found my telephone

number while exploring the Discipleship Ministries website and had some questions about Covenant Discipleship. I answered her questions about Covenant Discipleship groups and then told her how the groups' mission includes forming women and men as leaders in discipleship who help the congregation faithfully carry out its disciple-making mission. We had a lively conversation until I described the office of class leaders. There was a long silence, and then I heard her softly sobbing. She gathered herself and came back on the line to explain her tears.

Three years before calling me, she was in a *Disciple* Bible study class in her home church in Dubuque. During the course of the thirty-four-week study of the Bible and discipleship, she discerned God calling her to serve him in the church. She prayed about the experience, and the call just would not go away. She met with her pastor and told about how she believed God was calling her to service in the church.

The pastor did what every pastor is trained to do. She told the woman that if God is calling, then she should go to licensing school and enroll in the course of study to become a licensed local pastor. The pastor assumed that if God calls a woman or man to ministry, then God was calling that person to serve as a pastor.

The woman continued her story and told me how she went to licensing school, her bishop appointed her to a three-point charge, and then she enrolled in the course of study at Saint Paul School of Theology in Kansas City. But she never felt like serving as a pastor was really what God called her to. She couldn't help feeling like she did not belong in that role. When I explained the office of class leader, she realized what God's call was for her. She knew God called her to be a leader in discipleship for the people in her home congregation. God did not call her to serve as a pastor. God called her to the office of class leader with the people of her home congregation.

The pastor in this case is not at fault. I say this because the office of class leader has been absent from United Methodist consciousness for over one hundred years. When a person tells her pastor or a member of the congregation that she believes God is calling her, the natural course of action is to assume that God is calling her to ordained ministry, either as an elder, a deacon, or a local pastor. I am convinced that many women and men serving as pastors today were actually called by God to the office of class leader. They are doing their best to be faithful to Christ and his church. But they are struggling with always feeling that their gifts and call do not quite fit the work they are appointed to do.

If The United Methodist Church were to once again embrace and deploy the office of class leader and other lay offices (lay servant, lay speaker, lay leader, certified lay minister) and understand that God calls various persons to a variety of offices, including that of ordained elder or deacon, then we could more effectively help candidates discern their call.

The call to serve God and the church is both internal and external. You need to listen to both what God is saying to your heart and to what God is saying to you through others who know you. Most important are the internal promptings. For some, it is like hearing a voice from God speaking to their heart. You know such promptings, voices, and feelings are real because if they are of God they will not let go. The feelings and promptings will stay with you and will not let up until you surrender.

For class leaders, the beginnings of God's call to serve will come through your experience of your Covenant Discipleship group. Participating in the weekly meetings and striving to be more intentional about living the Christian life shaped by the General Rule of Discipleship opens your heart to grace in new ways. You will perceive God nudging you when new opportunities to serve come your way or when you lead prayer or take responsibility for a service project for the first time. The discipline of the Covenant Discipleship group will open your heart, soul, and mind to perceive God's call upon your life. He will supply the grace you need to respond to that call. You need to know that if God is calling you, he will not stop calling until you stop resisting and surrender.

The external call comes from the people God puts in your life. The most obvious will be when your pastor invites you to consider serving as a class leader. The invitation will be reinforced by members of your Covenant Discipleship group.

The external call is further reinforced during the discernment process with the committee on nominations and leader development and the pastor. It continues when the charge conference meets to consider your intention to be commissioned and to serve as a class leader.

> If you are hesitating to accept the office of class leader because you don't feel qualified, the most important question to ask yourself is not whether you feel adequate for the job, or whether you think you can measure up to the standards of faithful discipleship. The question is much more basic. Never mind how well you think you are doing in your discipleship, or how badly, is following Jesus Christ what you really *want* to do? If the answer to this question is yes, then your best will be good enough for Christ.
>
> What is more, you will be helping some of your fellow church members who likewise want to do their best as Christian disciples, but feel that their faith is inadequate, or the task is beyond their abilities. Through your work as a class leader, you can reassure them that their best is indeed good enough for Jesus, who understands their strengths and their weaknesses better than they themselves.[20]

Conclusion

John Wesley made disciples the way Paul did: "Brothers and sisters, join in imitating me, and observe those who live according to the example you have in us. . . . Keep on doing the things that you have learned and received and heard and seen in me, and the God of peace will be with you" (Phil. 3:17; 4:9). He led people to faith in Christ by placing them in small groups led by seasoned disciples who led by example. Class leaders taught the people in their classes new habits that opened their hearts to grace and the Holy Spirit. The Methodists learned how to live the Christian life by imitating their class leader. The class leaders served as role models, encouragers, and discipleship coaches. Class leaders are essential to the church's mission. They were the disciples of Jesus Christ who discipled their peers.

Today class leaders work as missional partners with their pastor. They are experienced disciples of Jesus Christ, called by God and given the gifts needed "to equip the saints for the work of ministry, for building up the body of Christ" (Eph. 4:12). They are women and men who love Jesus, obey his teachings, and believe his good news of the present and promised reign of God. They live as citizens of God's kingdom of love and justice and, therefore, are leaders in discipleship for the congregation. Class leaders are the pillars that support the congregation in its disciple-making mission. Congregations that commission and deploy class leaders understand the baptismal covenant that says the people, not the pastor, are responsible for work of disciple-making. The pastor's role is to preach Christ and his gospel, administer the sacraments, and order the life of the congregation to equip members to join Christ in God's mission in the world. Class leaders are partners in mission with the pastor to help the congregation do all in its power to increase faith, confirm hope, and perfect one another in love.

> The whole point of shared leadership in discipleship . . . is not doctrinal instruction or theological uniformity, but *application to the task in hand:* acts of compassion, justice, worship, and devotion. In equipping their congregations to follow this General Rule of Discipleship, pastors will find that their most natural support group has been there all the time—leaders who have been waiting to be asked to give a hand. In fact, they have been waiting for several generations.
>
> —David Lowes Watson
> *Forming Christian Disciples,* p. 134

CHAPTER 7

Introducing Class Leaders to the Congregation

The process of introducing class leaders to the congregation begins when Covenant Discipleship groups are introduced. The congregation and its key leadership need to understand that the goal of Covenant Discipleship groups is to form leaders in discipleship and to equip the congregation to make disciples of Jesus Christ who join his mission in the world. Some, but certainly not all, Covenant Discipleship group members will respond to the call to serve as class leaders.[1]

First Steps

During the first two years begin the process with these steps:

- During the pilot year, inform the congregation and its elected leaders about the office of class leader.
- Invite congregation members to prayerfully consider participating in a class of fifteen to twenty fellow members with a class leader who will help them with their discipleship, shaped by the General Rule of Discipleship.
- Adopt the General Rule of Discipleship as the congregation's rule of life.[2] Print it in the worship bulletin every Sunday, in the church newsletter, and on the congregation's website and

social media pages and profiles. Encourage both children and
adults to memorize it.

- Preach an annual sermon series interpreting the General Rule
  of Discipleship to the congregation. Encourage Sunday school
  classes to invite Covenant Discipleship group members to
  study and discuss the General Rule with them.
- Organize the confirmation class as a Covenant Discipleship
  group.

After the second year of Covenant Discipleship groups, most
members will have heard the General Rule several times. It will be
familiar to them when the process of introducing class leaders and
classes begins.

There is no hard and fast rule for introducing class leaders after
two years. Context and pastoral judgment will determine the timing
for the congregation. Class leaders and classes will likely be very new
and unknown to most members and congregational leaders. Very
few, if any, will have any knowledge or memory of class leaders serving in the church. Allow time to teach and prepare them to accept
the idea of laypeople serving as discipleship coaches, helping their
peers to live as Christian disciples. Take as long as needed to gain
members' acceptance.

Be prepared for resistance. Some will resist this method of peer-
to-peer coaching for discipleship. Unfortunately, very little is done
to combat the individualism people bring with them into the church;
not only individualism but also the notion of appointed, seminary-
trained clergy as being the "professional Christians" who are the
experts paid to make disciples.

I once helped introduce Covenant Discipleship groups to a subur-
ban United Methodist congregation. I helped them understand that
the goal of the groups was to form leaders in discipleship for the
congregation, and some would serve as class leaders. I then gave a
lengthy description of the work of a class leader. At the conclusion of
the presentation I asked, "What do you think would happen to this
congregation and its mission if you had active Covenant Discipleship

groups and class leaders?" After a long pause, one at the men at the end of the table spoke up and said, "No way! I don't see it happening, because there's only one person in this room who is qualified to help me with my discipleship. That's Pastor Charlotte here. But I'm not sure I want her to do that for me."

Everyone in the room agreed with their friend's response. They were uncomfortable with the idea of a fellow member of the congregation helping with their discipleship. They agreed that the only person in the congregation qualified to talk to them about discipleship was their seminary-trained, ordained pastor. I have encountered similar comments in numerous other congregations. This has convinced me that the church, and the dominant culture, has thoroughly convinced people to believe that faith and discipleship are private. "It's no one's business but mine and Jesus'." The religious professionals are the only people "qualified" to discuss such matters.

A good way to begin to counter such resistance is through teaching, preaching, and faithful interpretation of the baptismal covenant, discipleship, and the meaning of church membership (see ¶¶217–21 in *The Book of Discipline of The United Methodist Church*). Help people understand that scripture and tradition teach that faith and discipleship are deeply personal relationships with Christ. But that relationship is not private. Christ calls us into the community of the church, because we experience and receive grace through relationships with the people who are marked with his name: Christian. As John Wesley famously wrote,

> Christianity is essentially a social religion; and that to turn it into a solitary religion, is indeed to destroy it.
>
> By Christianity I mean that method of worshipping God which is here revealed to man by Jesus Christ. When I say, This is essentially a social religion, I mean not only that it cannot subsist so well, but that it cannot subsist at all, without society,—without living and conversing with other *people*. And in showing this, I shall confine myself to those considerations which will arise from the very discourse before us. But

if this be shown, then doubtless, to turn this religion into a solitary one is to destroy it.[3]

Some Christians are so thoroughly formed by individualism in the dominant culture that it will take time to convince them. Loving persistence, patience, and faithfulness to follow Christ in the world is the best response.

Official Proposal

During the summer of the second year, after the pilot year and at the time the groups are opened to the congregation, submit a formal proposal to the church council, for example:

> We propose to recruit class leaders from the Covenant Discipleship groups for commissioning by the congregation. Each class leader will be assigned a class of fifteen to twenty members of the congregation. Class leaders will help members of his or her class with their discipleship, shaped by the General Rule of Discipleship.

The purpose of the official proposal is for the church council to consider, discuss, and approve the formal proposal and take it to the annual charge conference or church conference.

After the council approves the proposal, the pastor and committee on nominations and leader development begin recruiting three to five members of the Covenant Discipleship groups to serve as class leaders. These people will be presented to the charge or church conference in autumn. The summer months will allow time for recruiting class leaders for the pilot classes, which will begin after the annual Covenant Sunday in early January. David Lowes Watson writes, "This brings the issue before the whole congregation and gives an opportunity for the widest possible approval. For the same reason, the congregation may wish to make this a church conference rather than a charge conference in order to extend the vote to all church members who wish to attend."[4]

Recruiting Class Leaders

Many candidates for class leaders will come from the Covenant Discipleship groups. They exhibit maturity in faith and discipleship, they faithfully attend their Covenant Discipleship group, and members of their group and the congregation look to them as trustworthy role models.

Do not expect everyone in a Covenant Discipleship group to become a class leader. Only those who have the time and energy and who feel called will respond to the invitation to serve. The commitment is to serve one year at a time. Class leaders are commissioned annually. It is up to them to choose how long they want to serve.

The search for class leaders should extend beyond Covenant Discipleship groups. Watson advises,

> Indeed, anyone who has shown intentionality about her or his discipleship is a prospective class leader. Those who are serious about serving Jesus Christ in the world, never mind how much they themselves still have to learn, are the ones who can best be trusted to lead others in their walk with Christ. Even if someone has tended to focus on one aspect of discipleship to the neglect of other duties and responsibilities of the Christian life, that is no reason to discount this person's potential as a class leader. Participation in a covenant discipleship group will quickly balance one's leadership with all the dimensions of the General Rule.[5]

Expectations of Class Leaders

Class leaders should be authentic Christian disciples, accepting of others, courteous yet candid, and blameless in their lives.

1. *Class leaders should be authentic Christian disciples. Authentic* here means a person whose faith is seen by others to be sincere and genuine. She is not going through the motions in order to be seen by others. An authentic Christian disciple is acquainted with

repentance from sin and knows his dependence upon grace in order to live as one who is forgiven. She is a Christian who "professes to pursue [in whatsoever measure she has attained] holiness of heart and life, inward and outward conformity in all things to the revealed will of God."[6] He habitually practices the means of grace and is eager to initiate others to join him. Watson says,

> But most of all, an authentic Christian disciple is one who knows what it is to strive for obedience to Jesus Christ in the midst of worldly temptations and in spite of countless failures. This knowledge cannot be learned secondhand. It can only be gained by following Jesus Christ, doing the best one can with the grace one is given, and knowing more and more with the passing years that Christ is all in all.
>
> Persons who have this knowledge have the ring of authenticity in their witness to Jesus Christ and the mark of authenticity in their walk with Jesus Christ. They do not merely know *about* Jesus Christ. They *know* Jesus Christ.[7]

2. *Class leaders should be accepting of others.* Mature disciples understand that people come to faith in a variety of ways and stages of life. They are open to the faith and experience of others, recalling their own ups and downs in their discipleship. They do not expect others to all think or believe as they do. Class leaders are open to learning from others and listen to their stories and experiences without judgment but in a spirit of grace and love. According to Watson, "Their own spiritual pilgrimage renders them unwilling and unable to pass judgment on anyone else's response to God's grace—whatever that response might be. This in turn enables them to be a guide and mentor to everyone."[8]

3. *Class leaders should be courteous yet candid.* David Lowes Watson writes, "The purpose of the office of class leader is not to shepherd church members, nor yet to provide them with pastoral care. These are important ministries of the church for which there are leaders already in place and some excellent resources available.

Class leaders are more concerned with grounding the discipleship of other church members—showing them the ropes, giving them suggestions for the basics of Christian living in the world, and making sure that their discipleship is balanced according to the General Rule of compassion, justice, worship, and devotion."[9]

4. *Class leaders should be blameless in their lives.* Class leaders will be persons looked up to by others in the congregation. People will observe the way they conduct themselves in the church and in public. This is one reason the person needs to be blameless in his or her daily life. People need to see coherence between the life in Christ the person professes to live and the person's behavior in church, in public, and at home. This is not to say that unrealistic scrutiny be placed on class leaders. But others need to see them as sincere and trustworthy in all things.[10]

Piloting Class Leaders

Given that classes and class leaders are likely very new approaches to the congregation's disciple-making mission, plan a pilot year for class leaders. Your initial efforts at recruiting class leaders will more than likely result in a small number of candidates. An equally small number of members will respond positively to being part of a class and having a discipleship coaching relationship with a class leader. The best course of action is to use the first year or two as a pilot project. Give the congregation, class members, and class leaders time to try on accountable discipleship and learn from the experience.

In David Watson's experience, "a pilot process can do much to allay anxieties. By showing how an accountable discipleship is not only the most faithful but ultimately the most rewarding form of Christian living in the world, and by showing people step-by-step how pilot classes can help them to form such a discipleship, pilot class leaders will gain acceptance for the office with much more integrity. They will stimulate interest among church members in a positive and non-threatening way; and they will avoid the imposition of a pastoral superstructure—the last thing we need today in the church. Piloting class leaders means that the office will take root in congregations."[11]

The pilot process will give the new class leaders on-the-job training for their new position. "For the fact of the matter is that being a class leader does not require intensive training. Showing people the ropes merely requires the experience of having used the ropes first. The General Rule of Discipleship is not complicated. Acts of compassion, justice, worship, and devotion are very straightforward, and can readily be demonstrated to other people—provided, of course, that one is doing them oneself."[12]

Annual Commissioning of Class Leaders

Class leaders are appointed annually by the charge conference. This ensures that the congregation participates in and is invested in the success of class leaders and class members in their care. It provides a means for annual evaluation of effectiveness and determining the willingness of the class leader to serve. The hope is that class leaders will take on the ministry as a lifetime vocation and provide the congregation with a wealth of missional experience. The annual process "reaffirms the accountability of the class leaders to the congregation as a whole."[13]

The appointed class leaders should be commissioned to their office during a Sunday morning worship service. "An Order for the Commissioning of Class Leaders" is found in appendix K of this book and in *The United Methodist Book of Worship* (p. 602). A good time for this is during the annual Covenant Renewal Service, held each January. This is also the most appropriate time to renew and recognize Covenant Discipleship groups and invite members of the congregation to join existing groups or form new groups. Invite groups to present their covenants to the congregation as a sign of their commitment to lead in its disciple-making mission. You will find an order of dedication in appendix J.

Provide all class leaders a copy of this book to study with the pastor. This will help prepare them for their work as their class is formed.

The Leaders' Meeting

After class leaders have been appointed by the charge conference, the monthly leaders' meeting must be established. Hold this meeting on a Saturday morning with breakfast. This is an essential element of the class leader ministry, because it establishes partnership with the appointed pastor or pastoral staff. Class leaders are partners with the pastor in the disciple-making mission of the congregation. They extend the General Rule of Discipleship into the congregation, enabling the congregation to disciple many more people than if this work was left to the pastor alone. As Watson states, "Each meeting has two objectives: to provide ongoing support and supervision for the class leaders; and to 'take the pulse' of the congregation through the reports of the class leaders. While there need be no set agenda, these two objectives should always be given regular attention, and will normally comprise most of what is discussed."[14]

In the meeting, class leaders receive the support they need from the pastor. He or she establishes a collegial relationship with class leaders as partners in the congregation's mission. This is done through regular affirmation of class leaders and their ministry. The pastor supports them through prayer and occasional teaching and training in pastoral skills such as active listening, asking open-ended questions, meeting and accepting people where they are, and honoring the faith they have in order to help them to grow in their pursuit of holiness of heart and life.

The meeting is also an opportunity for the pastor to keep class leaders regularly informed about the congregation's programs and activities. This information is important for class leaders to have in order to guide members of their classes to appropriate opportunities to intentionally practice the General Rule of Discipleship. They can direct class members to a Bible study, small group, outreach program, or special events that helps them to be more connected to the congregation and to grow in their discipleship.

The leaders' meeting also serves as a way for the pastor to take the pulse of the congregation. Class leaders will contact more members of the congregation than any pastor can ever visit. They help the pastor know more clearly the state of the member's spiritual and missional involvement. Without breaking confidences, class leaders may also make the pastor aware of members who may need extra pastoral attention. In addition, Watson notes,

> Just as important as learning about members' problems, the leaders' meeting can be a means of discovering a congregation's gifts and graces. Class leaders are going to acquire considerable knowledge in this regard as they help shape the discipleship of their members around the General Rule. In directing their classes toward the ongoing activities of the congregation, and in encouraging them to participate, they will gain a sense of what church members really need in order to develop their walk with Christ.
>
> By sharing these insights at the leader's meeting, they can help the pastoral staff and the church council to plan church programs that address genuine needs and interests, rather than try to discover what will attract people's participation—or worse, using up reserves of goodwill in persuading people to support unnecessary and unwanted activities.[15]

How to Form and Care for Classes

The following section contains important material explaining how to form and care for classes. The material is reproduced here from Forming Christian Disciples: The Role of Covenant Discipleship and Class Leaders in the Congregation *(pp. 158–67) with the author's permission.*

Forming the Classes

Once the leaders' meeting is functioning, its first major task is to assign a group of church members to each class leader. These missional groupings will be known as *classes*; and since this is a common word in the church, it is important to be clear about their nature and purpose.

We noted earlier that when class leaders and class meetings were introduced into early Methodism, class leaders were appointed first and were then assigned classes. The sequence is significant, because it indicated that these subdivisions of the early Methodist societies were not so much a small group strategy as a means of implementing leadership. Small group dynamics quickly developed, of course, as the weekly gatherings fostered a spirit of "watching over one another in love." But the classes were formed around the class leaders, and not vice versa, because the purpose of the early class meetings was the fostering of an obedient discipleship. The fellowship that followed was a blessing, not an objective.

Classes, Not Class Meetings

In assigning classes to class leaders we must keep that purpose clearly in view, because in the average United Methodist congregation of today it will not be necessary to convene the classes as class meetings. It may even be counterproductive to do so, at least for quite some time.

This may seem to part with the tradition we have been at such pains to recover. It may also seem to reject the experience of those branches of Methodism where the tradition of class leaders and class meetings has been kept alive. But in fact it is merely to take note of the transition in North American Methodism from small societies to a large pluralistic church, and also to accept the reality of our present cultural context in the United States.

With regard to our history, we have already noted that when Methodism became a church, the role of the class leader gradually changed from leading in discipleship to pastoring a subdivision of the congregation. We should also note that the class meeting underwent a similar change. As Methodist congregations grew in size, they found it increasingly difficult to hold to the disciplines of the early societies, and class meetings began to adopt a less demanding agenda. Rather than

accountability for the practice of discipleship, the weekly
gatherings focused on prayer and testimony, a format that
ultimately became stereotyped and then sterile.

This is a timely warning for the church of today, where
discipleship is often confused with Christian fellowship,
particularly where small groups are concerned. When the
objective is accountable discipleship, then the early Methodist class meeting provides an excellent small group model, as
in present-day covenant discipleship groups. Such groups are
for those who are ready to take their discipleship seriously—
persons who are always in a minority. Covenant discipleship
groups in a congregation rarely consist of more than 15 percent of the active members, or 5 to 7 percent of the membership roll.

Classes for Discipleship

On the other hand, when the objective is to help the church
membership as a whole to grow in their discipleship, then it is
questionable whether the small group format is necessary or
even appropriate. Given the wide range of Christian commitment to be found in the average North American congregation, it is unlikely that a common focus on the General Rule
of Discipleship could be sustained in a representative small
group. There would be too much disparity, too many different concerns, and the result would almost certainly be to
opt for a less demanding agenda—precisely what led to the
demise of the old class meeting.

Besides this, there are countless other small group activities in congregations today. There are prayer groups, Bible
study groups, book and issue study groups, service groups,
affinity groups, to name but a few. Indeed, therein lies the most
dangerous pitfall of trying to reintroduce class meetings along
with class leader: They would be seen as just another small
group activity—the last thing most church members want or
need. Instead of extending the General Rule of Discipleship

throughout a congregation, class meetings would be seen as an imposition. Their purpose would be thwarted.

By contrast, if classes can be assigned to class leaders without the necessity of being convened, but merely as missional groupings, class leaders will have the freedom and flexibility to help the members with their discipleship, one-on-one, at whatever stage of the Christian journey a member happens to be. The member will be aware that by accepting assignment to such classes they can be provided with some basic assistance in their daily walk with Christ.

They will also know that their class leaders are persons whose chief qualification for the job is that they are leading the way, not by superior accomplishment, but by holding themselves accountable week by week in a covenant discipleship group. In a word, they will know that their class leaders are trustworthy, and that their guidance can be accepted in full confidence.

Discipleship Classes and Sunday School Classes

Another reason for not convening these discipleship classes is that the word *class* is chiefly associated in the United States today with church school or Sunday school—a place where everyone from infants to senior citizens can learn about the Christian faith and at the same time experience a direct and often intimate form of Christian community.

The classes to be assigned to class leaders clearly have a very different purpose. They will be classes for the forming of Christian discipleship, rather than instruction in the faith or assimilation into the congregation. Yet if they were to be convened as class meetings along with the office of class leader, they would be seen as a duplication of much that is already taking place in the Sunday school, and could well cause friction and divided loyalty among faithful church members.

The office of class leader, on the other hand, can readily be revitalized without disturbing the adult classes of the Sunday school, any more than it will disturb the other programmatic and administrative dimensions of the congregation. The classes assigned to class leaders will be complementary to existing church organizations; and far from tampering or interfering with what is already in place, classes and class leaders will be a tremendous source of strengthening and reinvigoration.

Assigning the Classes

The recommended number of persons to be assigned to each class leader is fifteen to twenty. This is not a hard and fast rule, however, and the size of classes can be determined by the leaders' meeting in consultation with the church council. There are no criteria for class membership, other than the willingness of the person to accept the guidance of the class leader, and that of the leader to accept the person into his or her class.

The assigning of members to the classes should be done carefully, and by no means all at once. We have already noted that the first class leaders will probably be in the nature of a pilot project, and will therefore be too few in number for the whole congregation to be assigned initially. Likewise it may well take time for church members to respond in sufficient numbers to constitute full classes for all the class leaders appointed.

In either event, classes should be formed only as members are willing to accept assignment to the class leaders available. It will take several leaders' meetings to make assignments and reassignments, as prospective members accept or decline, and the process should not be hurried. If it means a modest beginning, that is preferable by far to a superimposed network of leaders and classes, neither of whom are fully aware of what they ought to be doing, and both of whom are thus likely to have a negative experience.

1. Make each class as representative as possible of the membership as a whole.

It will be a pastoral temptation to assign the first classes on the basis of "problem members," or "inactives," or "seasoned resisters." This would be a serious mistake. The purpose of class leaders is to develop and strengthen the discipleship of the whole congregation, and each class should be as representative as possible of the full range of the membership.

2. Special factors may govern the forming of classes if this assists the work of the class leaders.

There may well be special factors which make the assignment of certain members to a class leader more practicable or feasible: neighborhood groupings, for example, or familiarity with the leader in another setting, such as a Sunday school class or a Bible study group. The leaders' meeting should feel free to assign classes in this way—provided the special factors do not exclude anyone from such a class.

3. Assign all new church members to a class leader.

A good way to develop the office of class leader is to begin assigning all new members to a class when they join. As they take their membership vows and are welcomed into the fellowship of the church, their new class leader can stand with them, and be recognized by the congregation. It should be made clear on such occasions that class leaders are not the same as the "fellowship friends" or "shepherds" with whom congregations often pair new church members for a few months to make them feel at home. Ministries of this nature are important, and should remain in place. The relationship with a class leader is very different, however, and the welcome extended to new members provides an opportunity for the pastor to inform the congregation accordingly.

*4. Invitations to join a class should be extended by class
leaders in person.*

As the leaders' meeting determines the assignment of classes,
invitations to join a class should be extended to each member
by the class leader concerned.

Of course, there are bound to be refusals. However carefully the assignment process has taken into account the attitudes of prospective class members, there will be resistance,
for any number of reasons. These refusals should be accepted
graciously by the class leader, but without conceding the
value and purpose of forming the classes—nor should the
leader feel personally rejected. We are dealing here with the
retuning of muscle in the church, the reactivation of that part
of the body that gives it strength. As with all muscle that has
not been used for a while, there will be resistance—and in
due course, some aches and pains as well.

On the other hand, when a church member agrees to
accept the invitation and join a class, the spiritual affirmation experienced by the leader is one of the highest privileges
of the Christian life. The knowledge that someone else is
willing to benefit from one's own walk with Christ, and the
assurance that God's grace is indeed at work in the ministry
and mission of the congregation, prove to be immeasurable
blessings.

Furthermore, the forming of these classes marks the
beginning of relationships that in many instances will last a
lifetime. We know this for sure, because there are biographi-
cal accounts from our Methodist forebears that bear just
such a testimony.

*5. Do not give up on members who are not initially receptive
to the idea of having a class leader.*

As we have noted, it will take much advocacy and much persistence to inform and educate the congregations of today
about the nature and purpose of class leaders and classes.

Not only are there many Methodists who have no memory of class leaders; there are not many members of United Methodist congregations who were not originally Methodist.

The leaders' meeting should regularly discuss ways and means of extending the number of classes and class leaders. Invitations to join classes should be repeated, many times, and when least expected there will be a positive response. Likewise, every opportunity should be taken to show how class leaders are enriching the life and work of the congregation. At council and committee meetings, in Sunday school classes, and above all in the worship of the church, the office should be given visibility and affirmation.

Even so, there will be times when the congregation seems to be impervious, and the pilot process seems to be interminable. At such times, the leaders' meeting should be used to help leaders remember that they themselves have accepted the office, and are convinced that it is a means of grace. They have come to know that "watching over each other in love" is a method of forming faithful disciples and vital congregations, and that grace is indeed at work throughout the membership. As with all seed planted in good ground, it will be slower to grow than that which is planted in shallow ground. But it will also bear fruit when the other has long since withered (Matt. 13:3-8).

6. Be open to the possibility of class meetings.

While much has been made in this chapter of the contextual factors that make it unwise for class leaders in the average United Methodist congregation to convene their classes as class meetings, this is not to say that such meetings should be avoided. On the contrary, the ideal situation for any large church would be for all members to meet regularly in a group to be accountable for their discipleship, and that all members would be willing to make the sort of commitment to be found in covenant discipleship groups. Such a church would be truly revolutionary—as indeed is the case in places where such discipleship is practiced.

The reality of The United Methodist Church is very far from this. In a large, inclusive, pluralistic church, only a few members are willing to make such a commitment. And in the present climate of individualism in North America, the great majority of church members will engage in group activities only to the extent that they themselves are helped. They are rarely willing to enter into Christian community as a means of improving their discipleship.

Even so, the reintroduction of class leaders can be an important step in this direction. At first, and for quite some time, classes will have to be regarded as a missional grouping of individuals, each member having a personal relationship with the class leader. But in due course, there may well be a desire on the part of some, or even all of the members, to have a meeting together, to share mutual experiences and to provide mutual support.

Class leaders should be ready for this opportunity, and should take full advantage of it.

Class Leaders and Other Church Officers

Once they are introduced, a crucial aspect of the credibility of class leaders will be to clarify their relationship to other church leaders. Their direct link with the pastor, to say nothing of their appointment by charge conference, is sure to raise questions about the extent to which their responsibilities might duplicate or even conflict with those of other church officers.

The most important clarification is that class leaders provide a *complementary* role in the congregation. It is helpful in this regard to return to the distinction between transactional and transformational leadership. Transactional leadership is responsible for meeting the needs of church members, and for the institutional maintenance of the church. Transformational leadership is responsible for keeping church members focused on the vision of the gospel and the obligations of their discipleship. This is not to say that these two leadership roles are mutually exclusive. Even the most fastidious chairperson of trustees can find a prophetic voice, and even the most visionary pastor has to deal with air conditioning. But it is to say that the two modes of leadership must be given distinct and equal emphasis in the life and work of the church.

In most congregations today the transactional mode of leadership predominates to the neglect of the transformational. Yet the answer to this imbalance does not lie in trying to make administrative and programmatic leaders more transformational. Their mode of leadership must be transactional, because they are responsible for running the church and meeting members' needs. Their energies are already expended in doing precisely that.

Class leaders, by contrast, have the freedom to function in a transformational mode. They are responsible for helping church members grow in their obedience to Jesus Christ. They are also responsible for directing them toward the resources they need in order to live out their discipleship in the world. In this way, they are fully complementary to the transactional leadership of the church.

On the one hand, class leaders need the administrative and programmatic dimensions of the congregation in order to resource their classes. Without these, the General Rule of Discipleship remains skeletal. On the other hand, they enrich the life and work of the congregation by involving their class members more intentionally in its ministry and mission. If there is any overlap, it is by way of reinforcing everyone else's work.

Ex Officio Membership

This means that class leaders must not only be aware of everything that is going on in the programmatic life of the congregation: they must also be welcomed as significant new colleagues. We recommend that class leaders be *ex officio* members of the church council. However, their leadership role will be greatly enhanced if all committees and task forces of the congregation invite a representative class leader to serve *ex officio* with them. And all leadership roles in the church will be further enhanced if other church officers will consult regularly with the class leaders about their respective responsibilities.

Such a sharing of information and insights will have many advantages. To begin with, it will mutually enrich the leadership of the church. Class leaders will be better informed about opportunities for the involvement of their class members; and committees, commissions, and task groups will be better supported in their work. Likewise, class leaders will bring the insights of their classes to business and program meetings—classes that are widely representative of the congregation as a whole. In turn, they will impart to their class members a greater sense of involvement in the life and mission of the larger church—a church that is not only connectional, but worldwide.

The Lay Leader and Class Leaders

In this regard, there is one church officer with whom class leaders should have an especially close relationship, and that is the congregation's lay leader. The titles of the two offices are very similar, and it is important to keep them distinct in the life and mission of the church. Yet they complement each other in very significant ways. The lay leader functions as the primary lay representative of the congregation, and has wide responsibilities for the fostering of lay ministry that will most effectively fulfill the church's mission. These responsibilities include membership on a number of key committees, and serving as interpreter to the congregation of the actions and programs of the general church. The office of class leader, on the other hand, is more directly focused on helping a missional subgrouping of the congregation to be formed in Christian discipleship.

Because they complement one another so directly, it is essential to have good communication between the two. Accordingly, the lay leader should be an *ex officio* member of the monthly leaders' meeting. By attending these meetings, the lay leader can be better informed about the congregation as a whole, and at the same time contribute an overview of the congregation that will help the class leaders in their work. Since the two offices are distinct, there is nothing to prevent the lay leader from being a class leader as well; though few people are likely to have the time for both responsibilities.

The Most Important Word: RECOGNITION

In the final analysis, the most important word in the reintroduction of class leaders is *recognition*: recognition by the pastor that leaders in discipleship are there in the congregation, waiting to be asked to join in the pastoring of the flock; recognition by the congregation that some of their own members are called to be their leaders in following Christ; and recognition by the class leaders themselves that God's call to this leadership role is one of the highest privileges and responsibilities of the Christian life.

If all of this is recognized, by pastor and people alike, then class leaders will begin to assume their proper place in the congregation; and the preceding guidelines, while helpful perhaps at first, will quickly be left behind. For the office of class leader is not new. It was proven in practice by our Methodist forebears; it continues in practice among many of our Methodist colleagues; and it is still present in the collective memory of a church that badly needs the methodical discipleship it once nurtured.

The question to be asked, therefore, as a congregation considers incorporating the office of class leader into its life and work, is not whether it will work, but whether it is right. There are countless Methodists, past and present, who have answered that question with a resounding "yes." May there be many others who now decide to join them.[16]

Conclusion

The mission of each United Methodist congregation is to make disciples of Jesus Christ for the transformation of the world. The baptismal covenant tells us what is needed:

> With God's help we will proclaim the good news and live according to the example of Christ.
>
> We will surround these persons with a community of love and forgiveness, that they may grow in their trust of God, and be found faithful in their service to others.
>
> We will pray for them, that they may be true disciples who walk in the way that leads to life.[17]

The baptismal covenant concludes with the "Commendation and Welcome." The pastor addresses the congregation saying: "Members of the household of God, I commend these persons to your love and care. Do all in your power to increase their faith, confirm their hope, and perfect them in love." This commendation tells the pastor and congregation the missional work of disciple making is the work of the people of the church. The pastor plays an important role by preaching the gospel so that it is good news for the church and the world, administering the sacraments and organizing the missional life of the congregation. The work of disciple making belongs to the laity working as partners with the pastor.

In the Wesleyan tradition class leaders are the women and men who serve as discipleship coaches the congregation needs to carry out its mission of making disciples of Jesus Christ who are equipped to join him and his mission in the world. The General Rule of Discipleship is a rule of life that guides them in their missional work: To witness to Jesus Christ in the world and to follow his teachings through acts of compassion, justice, worship, and devotion under the guidance of the Holy Spirit.

God has placed in each congregation the leaders needed to do the disciple-making mission. Paul identifies them as apostles, prophets, evangelists, pastors, and teachers the church needs "to equip the saints for the work of ministry, for building up the body of Christ" (Eph. 4:11-12). Covenant Discipleship groups prepare these leaders in discipleship by opening their hearts and minds to hear God's call to serve as a leader in discipleship. Some are called to the office of class leader. They are the disciples who make disciples by their example and encouragement.

Class leaders work as partners in disciple making with the pastor. They help the congregation to be faithful in its mission and free the pastor to do the work God has called her or him to do. A pastor who serves alongside a cohort of class leaders is better informed about the lives of the people he or she is appointed to serve. Therefore, the pastor will be a more effective leader and the congregation will be faithful to its mission of equipping Christians to join Christ and his mission in the world.

Congregations that want to make disciples of Jesus Christ for the transformation of the world need Covenant Discipleship groups and class leaders.

Provoke One Another to Love

Therefore, my friends, since we have confidence to enter the sanctuary by the blood of Jesus, by the new and living way that he opened for us through the curtain (that is, through his flesh), and since we have a great priest over the house of God, let us approach with a true heart in full assurance of faith, with our hearts sprinkled clean from an evil conscience and our bodies washed with pure water. Let us hold fast to the confession of our hope without wavering, for he who has promised is faithful. And let us consider how to provoke one another to love and good deeds, not neglecting to meet together, as is the habit of some, but encouraging one another, and all the more as you see the Day approaching.

—Hebrews 10:19-25

"In a Christian believer love sits upon the throne which is erected in the inmost soul; namely, love of God and man, which fills the whole heart, and reigns without a rival. In a circle near the throne are all holy tempers;—longsuffering, gentleness, meekness, fidelity, temperance;

and if any other were comprised in 'the mind which was in Christ Jesus.' In an exterior circle are all the works of mercy, whether to the souls or bodies of men. By these we exercise all holy tempers; by these we continually improve them, so that all these are real means of grace, although this is not commonly adverted to. Next to these are those that are usually termed works of piety;—reading and hearing the word, public, family, private prayer, receiving the Lord's Supper, fasting or abstinence. *Lastly, that his followers may the more effectually provoke one another to love, holy tempers, and good works, our blessed Lord has united them together in one body, the Church, dispersed all over the earth; a little emblem of which, of the Church universal, we have in every particular Christian congregation.*

"This is that religion which our Lord has established upon earth, ever since the descent of the Holy Ghost on the day of Pentecost. This is the entire, connected system of Christianity: And thus the several parts of it rise one above another, from that lowest point, the assembling ourselves together, to the highest, love enthroned in the heart. And hence it is easy to learn the comparative value of every branch of religion. Hence also we learn a Fifth property of true zeal: That as it is always exercised *en kalo*, in that which is good, so it is always proportioned to that good, to the degree of goodness that is in its object."[1]

In Sermon 92, "On Zeal," quoted above, John Wesley provides insight into how disciples of Jesus Christ are formed and equipped to join Christ's mission in the world. He is very clear that disciples are formed in Christian community, through relationships formed in small groups with other Christ followers. He believed Christ built the church for his followers to "more effectually provoke one another to love, holy tempers, and good works." Wesley's inspiration for this belief is Hebrews 10:24.

This is what the baptismal covenant means when the congregation promises

> With God's help we will proclaim the good news and live according to the example of Christ. We will surround *these*

persons with a community of love and forgiveness, that *they* may grow in *their* trust of God, and be found faithful in *their* service to others. We will pray for *them*, that *they* may be true disciples who walk in the way that leads to life.[2]

And when the congregation receives the admonition to "do all in your power to increase their faith, confirm their hope, and perfect them in love," it means the congregation is organized to encourage and equip members to "more effectually provoke one another to love, holy tempers, and good works."

The dictionary provides the following definitions of "provoke:"

1. Make someone feel angry
2. Elicit response
3. Stir somebody to emotion
4. Incite something
5. Cause activity

The first four definitions are likely what comes immediately to mind when you hear the word *provoke*. It is typically used to describe negative feelings or actions. The second and fifth definitions are what Wesley, and the writer of Hebrews, had in mind. Using *provoke* in the context of encouraging a people to act for love and justice gets our attention.

Wesley, and the writer of Hebrews, knew people need to be *provoked* to love because they are inhibited by sin. Sin distorts our habits of thought and behavior, turning them inward, directing them toward the self. It produces self-centered thinking and behavior. This is what the apostle Paul writes about when he uses the term "works of the flesh." Sin convinces us to believe we are the center of the universe. Our needs and desires are all that matter. Paul describes works of the flesh: "fornication, impurity, licentiousness, idolatry, sorcery, enmities, strife, jealousy, anger, quarrels, dissensions, factions, envy, drunkenness, carousing" (Gal. 5:19-21). Works of the flesh come naturally. They are instinctive because "all have sinned and fall short of the glory of God" (Rom. 3:23).

When people enter the church through the waters of baptism they take the first step of new life in Christ and his household. The congregation's part of the covenant is to provide the means for members to keep the promises and help them to cooperate with the Holy Spirit working in them to overcome sin and the damage it has done.

The "fruit of the Spirit" are the outcome of the faith working through love. When Christians cooperate with the Holy Spirit and "provoke one another to love" they help one another live the baptismal covenant by working out their salvation (Phil. 2:12-13). The "works of the flesh" are overcome by "love, joy, peace, patience, kindness, generosity, faithfulness, gentleness, and self-control" (Gal. 5:22-23). The "fruit of the Spirit" are the habits John Wesley called "holy tempers."

Wesley believed that holy tempers are formed in us as we participate in the life of the church and *habitually* practice the means of grace—works of piety *and* works of mercy.

Christians "provoke one another to love, holy tempers, and good works" when they meet weekly in small groups to give an account of their discipleship, give support, and pray for one another. Covenant Discipleship groups, class leaders, and the missional groupings called classes described in this book are essential to the church's disciple-making mission.

A Rule of Life for the Congregation

The General Rule of Discipleship, "To witness to Jesus Christ in the world, and to follow his teachings through acts of compassion, justice, worship, and devotion under the guidance of the Holy Spirit," is a contemporary summary of the General Rules. It gives a succinct summary of the balanced and varied discipleship described by Jesus in the Great Commandment (Matt. 22:37-39). It shapes the covenant that Covenant Discipleship groups write and use to guide their life in their work of mutual accountability and support for growth in holiness of heart and life. As groups engage in weekly accountability for discipleship, members are formed as leaders in discipleship that the congregation needs for its disciple-making mission.

When congregations adopt a rule of life to shape their missional life, they give members a compass heading for living the baptismal covenant. The baptismal covenant, rule of life, and network of small groups where members provoke one another to love and good works equip members to join Christ and his mission in the world. The congregation cooperates with the dynamic of grace (prevenient, justifying, and sanctifying) and the Holy Spirit. It becomes a

> sign community of the coming reign of God. Pending the fullness of God's salvation, the task of the church, and of the Christian disciples who make up its work force, is to direct the world toward the kingdom which Jesus announced and inaugurated.
>
> To be a sign community means accepting that the mission of the church is in reality the mission of God, the work of the risen Christ and the Holy Spirit in the world. God's mission is nothing less than the gathering of the human family back home where they belong—home with God, now and for all eternity.
>
> If congregations are to be the sign communities Christ intended them to be, they must be subsumed by this hope and this vision. They must be so centered on the mission of God that those who belong to their company will be impelled into the world as messengers of God, servants of Jesus Christ, and channels of grace for the Holy Spirit.[3]

Charles Wesley beautifully describes Christ's vision for the church that exists as a sign community of the coming reign of God and equips its members to be channels of grace with Christ in the world:

> Help us to help each other, Lord,
> Each other's cross to bear;
> Let all their friendly aid afford,

And feel each other's care.

Touched by the lodestone of thy love,
Let all our hearts agree,
And ever toward each other move,
And ever move toward thee.[4]

The word *lodestone* is an eighteenth-century word for magnet. Wesley describes God's love as being like a magnet that draws us toward him. As you move closer and closer to God, you necessarily move closer and closer to your neighbor. The converse is also true: if you reject and move away from God, you put more distance between yourself and your neighbor. When congregations are centered in the life and mission of Jesus Christ, they provide the means for members to live the baptismal covenant by regularly provoking one another to love, holy habits, and good works. As love and trust grow among the people, they move closer and closer to God and one another, equipping them to be sent by God into the world to join Christ and his mission. The congregation becomes a sign community of the kingdom of God. It knows it is not the kingdom. But it knows where to find it. When visitors walk onto the church's property they immediately see and experience the one whose name and mission it represents.

APPENDIX A

Recommended Resources for Covenant Discipleship Group Members and Class Leaders

1. *A Disciple's Journal: A Guide for Daily Prayer, Bible Reading, and Discipleship.* This is a devotional resource designed for use by people in Covenant Discipleship groups. A new *Journal* is published annually before the first Sunday of Advent because it contains a daily lectionary based upon the Revised Common Lectionary. In addition to the daily Scripture lessons, excerpts from the works of John and Charles Wesley are provided for reading during each week of the year. Space is provided for Covenant Discipleship group members to record their acts of compassion, justice, worship, and devotion each week. Group members may bring the *Journal* with them to their weekly meeting.

2. The *Covenant Discipleship Connection* is a free monthly e-newsletter provided by Discipleship Ministries. It will appear in your e-mail inbox near the middle of each month. To subscribe go to http://umcdiscipleship.org/covenantdiscipleship and enter your e-mail address under "E-Newsletter Sign-up," found near the bottom of the left-hand column of the page.

3. "Covenant Discipleship Groups" brochures are a handy way to introduce people to the ministry. The brochures are available free from Discipleship Ministries. Request as many as you can use by sending an e-mail to cdgroups@umcdiscipleship.org. Please provide your name, church name, church address, and quantity of brochures you need.

4. The Covenant Discipleship page at the Discipleship Ministries website is filled with information and helps for Covenant Discipleship groups and class leaders. Go to http://umcdiscipleship. org/covenantdiscipleship.

5. The Covenant Discipleship lapel pin is a good gift for CD group members and class leaders. They may be ordered from the Upper Room online book store: bookstore.upperroom.org. Search for "Covenant Discipleship Lapel Pin."

6. Join the Covenant Discipleship group on Facebook to share ideas and experiences with others.

7. The Wesleyan Leadership blog is another good resource for information, inspiration, and ideas for Covenant Discipleship groups, class leaders, and pastors. Go to http://wesleyanleadership.com.

8. *The United Methodist Hymnal* contains the baptismal covenant, prayers, and hymns that Covenant Discipleship groups may use when they meet each week.

9. This book is based on the work of David Lowes Watson. It is helpful for group members to have access to his books, which are the foundation documents for Covenant Discipleship groups and class leaders today. You will find a list of his books in the bibliography.

APPENDIX B

Covenant Writing Helps

This appendix includes the following material to assist Covenant Discipleship groups in writing their covenants:

- two sample covenants
- sample covenant preambles
- sample covenant clauses
- sample covenant conclusions

Sample Covenant 1

In gratitude for the grace of Jesus Christ, in whose death we have died and in whose resurrection we receive new life, we pledge to be his disciples. We recognize that our time and talents are gifts from God, and we will use them to search out God's will for us and to obey. We will do our best not to compromise the will of God for human goals. We will serve both God and God's creation earnestly and lovingly. We respect and accept fully all group members, whose integrity and confidentiality we will uphold in all that we share. With God's grace and their help, we make this covenant.

I* will spend four hours each month helping the poor people in my community.

When I am aware of injustice to others, I will not remain silent.

I will obey the promptings of the Holy Spirit to serve God and my neighbor.

I will heed the warnings of the Holy Spirit not to sin against God and my neighbor.

I will worship each Sunday, unless prevented.

I will receive the sacrament of Holy Communion each week.

I will pray each day, privately and with family or friends.

I will read and study the scriptures each day.

I will return to Christ the first tenth of all I receive.

I will prayerfully care for my body and for the world in which I live.

I hereby make my commitment, trusting in the grace of God to give me the will and the strength to keep this covenant.

Date: _____ Signed: _____

* The use of the personal *I* or the collective *we* is entirely at the discretion of each group.

Sample Covenant 2

We are disciples of Jesus Christ. God intends to save us from sin and for lives of love to God and neighbor. God has called us and the Spirit has empowered us to be witnesses of God's kingdom and to grow in holiness all the days of our lives. We commit ourselves to use our time, skills, resources, and strength to love and serve God, neighbor, and creation, trusting God's power through these means to make us holy.

Acts of Compassion

I will seek out ways to show compassion for all people and all of God's creation.

Acts of Justice

I will witness for justice and encourage forgiveness always and reconciliation wherever possible.

I will support world peace with justice and communicate with elected representatives and others on these issues.

Acts of Worship

I will actively participate in corporate worship each week unless prevented.

I will offer my resources faithfully to support the work of God's kingdom, including the local congregation with which I am affiliated, with the tithe as my guide. (*Resources interpreted broadly to include money, time, and talents.*)

Acts of Devotion

I will spend time daily in reading scripture and offering prayer, including praying for enemies, and include the members of our Covenant Discipleship group in my daily prayers.

I will eat appropriately, get sufficient rest, exercise, and take at least one full day a week as sabbath.

> Open my eyes to your presence, O God,
>> that I may see the sorrows and joys of your creatures.
> Open my ears to your will, O God,
>> that I may have the strength to keep this covenant.
> Open my heart and my hands in mercy, O God,
>> that I may receive mercy when I fail. Amen.

Signed: _____ Date: _____

Sample Covenant Preambles

- Having been called by Jesus Christ to be disciples, with awe and trembling hearts, we answer his call to be Doorkeepers. This group shall exist for the purpose of support, communal prayer, receiving the Word, and watching over one another in love so that all are encouraged to work out their salvation and offer others Christ.
- Christian disciples need a firm foundation of faith. Paul urges the church at Ephesus to "grow up in every way into . . . Christ" so that they may "no longer be children tossed to and fro and blown about by every wind of doctrine. But speaking the truth in love, we must grow up in every way into him who is the head, into Christ" (Eph. 4:13-15, NRSV). To that end, that we may grow toward maturity of faith and celebrate God's presence with us and the gifts God has given us to use for service with Christ in the kingdom, we expect of all who join us . . .
- In gratitude for the grace of Jesus Christ, in whose death we have died and in whose resurrection we have found new life, we pledge to be his disciples. We recognize that our time and talents are gifts from God, and we will use them to search out God's will for us and to obey it.
- We will do our best not to compromise the will of God for human goals. We will serve both God and God's creation earnestly and lovingly. We respect and accept fully all group members, whose integrity and confidentiality we will uphold in all that we share. With God's grace and their help we covenant to . . .
- Called into being and empowered by the grace of God, we covenant to dedicate ourselves to a life that exemplifies Christ and the gospel. We offer our time, talents, abilities, and resources, in obedience to the gospel, acknowledging our dependence upon God's grace and the power of the Holy Spirit.
- Knowing that Jesus Christ died for me and that God calls me to be a disciple of Jesus Christ, I desire to practice the

following disciplines that I might know God's love, forgiveness, guidance, and strength. I desire to make God's will my own and to be obedient to it. I desire to remain in Christ with the help of this covenant so that I might bear fruit for the kingdom of God.

- To be a Christian disciple means sharing in Christ's ongoing work of salvation in the world. The task of discipleship therefore calls for the binding together of those with like mind and purpose, to "watch over one another in love." We covenant together to be present each week. We will open and close our meetings with prayer, to help focus our minds and hearts on God rather than on ourselves and our accomplishments. We will approach each other with honesty and in a spirit of love. Understanding that our purpose is not to judge each other, we will speak honestly—both in terms of our keeping the covenant as well as our failure to do so.

Sample Covenant Clauses

Acts of Compassion

- I will seek out people in need and do all I can to help them.
- We will strive to increase our service to others and graciously acknowledge others' service to us.
- I will spend one hour each week visiting a lonely person whom I would not ordinarily visit.
- I will spend four hours each month helping the disadvantaged in my community.
- We will balance the time we devote to school, church, work, family, and friends, including our own spiritual and recreational life.
- I will spend an hour each day with my children.
- I will spend some time each day with each member of my family in meaningful communication.
- We will practice listening to other people as a ministry of grace.

- I will express feelings of genuine appreciation to at least one person each day.
- We will each establish a meaningful relationship with someone in prison and, where possible, with their families.
- I will get to know at least one poor family.
- I will offer friendship each day to someone of an ethnic background different from my own.
- We will encourage our congregation in its missional giving, and do this by personal example.
- I will seek to help a family in need somewhere else in the world.
- I will eat one less meal each day and give the money to feed the hungry.

Acts of Justice

- When I am aware of injustices practiced in my church, my community, my nation, and the world, I will speak out.
- We will not be silent when confronted with social injustice.
- We will witness for justice, inclusiveness, and equality and will encourage reconciliation wherever possible.
- I will actively support a movement for world peace and will communicate regularly with my elected national representatives on issues of world peace.
- I will get to know at least one unemployed person, and I will communicate regularly with my elected local representatives on issues of unemployment and economic justice.
- I will get to know at least one person of a different ethnic background at my place of work.
- We will become more aware of social situations through attention to the news (newspapers, television, magazines, radio, websites).
- I will ask forgiveness of God each day for those who die of starvation, and I will work to alleviate world hunger.
- We will become an advocacy group for prisoners of religious and political conscience.

- We will devote our daily Bible study to the eighth-century prophets for the coming year.
- I will dissociate myself from racial slurs and jokes at my place of work.
- I will express disapproval of racial, social, and sexual prejudice among my relatives and friends.
- We will practice responsible stewardship of the world's resources in our personal lives and communal commitments.
- We will each take action to improve our relationship with our natural environment.
- I will strive for unconditional love and acceptance of all God's creations.

Acts of Worship

- I will be faithful in attendance and participation in worship each Sunday.
- I will receive the sacrament of Holy Communion each week, when possible in my Covenant Discipleship group.
- We will prayerfully consider what resources we can contribute to the work of Christ in the world.
- I will return to Christ the first tenth of all that I receive.
- We will pray for those who lead us in worship each week, and especially for the preacher.
- We will pray for those who visit our worship service, that they will be touched by grace.
- We will pray for those who are baptized in our church and visit the parents of baptized children.
- We will seek opportunities to worship with people of other races.
- I will develop the habit of worshiping three times a week: Sunday, Wednesday, and Friday.
- We will seek ways of bringing God's word alive during worship.
- We will seek to worship God in unexpected situations.
- We will attend and participate in healing services.

- I will pray earnestly for God to bless those who either enter our church or pass by its doors.

Acts of Devotion

- We will practice daily devotions, including the reading of scripture and prayer for group members.
- I will spend at least one hour each day in the disciplines of praise, thanksgiving, confession, petition, intercession and meditation.
- I will pray daily in solitude and with my family or friends. I will include all members of my Covenant Discipleship group in my daily prayers.
- I will keep a diary to plan my daily and weekly prayers.
- We will make the study of scripture a central part of our daily devotions.
- We will agree on our daily Bible readings and share our insights as we give an account each week.
- I will record spiritual insights from my daily Bible reading.
- I will read the Bible each day as a devotional exercise and not a study assignment.
- We will each keep a spiritual journal and will devote time at the end of each day to enter our reflections as the Holy Spirit leads us.
- I will spend at least thirty minutes each day alone with God, of which fifteen minutes will be spent just listening to God.
- I will pray each day for my enemies.
- I will take the initiative each day in holding family devotions.
- I will read only those materials and watch only those programs that enhance my discipleship.
- I prayerfully pledge to practice responsible stewardship of my God-given resources: my body, the environment, my artistic graces, and my intellectual gifts.

- In order to care for our individual wholeness in body, mind, and spirit, we will schedule time each week for retreat, reflection, renewal, and fun.
- Knowing that my body is the temple of God, I will prayerfully plan my work and leisure time.
- I will seek the guidance of the Holy Spirit in fasting.

Spiritual Guidance

- I will remember that whatever I do, be it work, study, or recreation, is dedicated to God.
- We will seek out ways to yield our all to God's saving grace.
- I will acknowledge whenever I disobey a spiritual prompting or fail to heed a spiritual warning.
- We will obey the prompting of the Holy Spirit to serve God and our neighbors.
- We will obey the warnings of the Holy Spirit to not sin against God or our neighbors.

Sample Covenant Conclusions

- Knowing that the grace of God works in each of us, I pray that my heart be opened to God's presence, that my eyes be opened to see the sorrows and joys of God's creatures, and that my ears be opened to hear God's will so that I will have the strength to keep this covenant with each of the other members.
- We therefore pledge our commitment to God and to the group, that the choices we make in our daily journeys will enhance our growth as Christians, honor our Creator and Redeemer, and minister to our world.
- Recognizing that there are times when we cannot live up to the standards we have set for ourselves, we covenant to support each other in an encouraging and constructive manner.

- Trusting in grace, we pledge to support each other as we leave the confines of comfort in our search to do God's will in the world.

Open our eyes to your presence, O God,
    that we may see the sorrows and joys or your creatures.
Open our ears to your will, O God,
    that we may have the strength to keep this covenant.
Open our hearts and our hands in mercy, O God,
    that we may receive mercy when we fail. Amen.

APPENDIX C

Revising a Covenant

The group covenant is not a static document. Its purpose is to center the group members in their daily witness to Jesus Christ in the world. As time passes and relationships develop within the group it's natural and expected that the discipleship of members will change and grow. If the covenant is going to meet the needs of the group, it too needs to change and grow.

- Do you have clauses that are routine for everyone in the group? That is, week after week everyone in the group reports doing that act of compassion, justice, worship or devotion.
- Do you have a clause the group regularly neglects? Is there a clause you and other members of the group either cannot or will not do?
- Does your covenant have a clause that is clumsy, outdated, unclear, or poorly written?
- As you read the covenant preamble do you feel it no longer reflects the character or goals of the group?

If you answered yes to any of these questions, then it's time to revise your group's covenant. A good place to begin is for the group to review chapter 4 of this book. This provides a helpful refresher on the purpose, character, and structure of the covenant. It is essential that the group keep the covenant revision process centered in Jesus Christ and shaped by the General Rule of Discipleship:

> To witness to Jesus Christ in the world and to follow his teachings through acts of compassion, justice, worship, and devotion under the guidance of the Holy Spirit.

Begin the process of revising your covenant by refamiliarizing the group with the General Rule. The General Rule and the group covenant are centered in Jesus and equipping his disciples to lead the church to participate in his mission for the world. They do this by helping disciples to form habits that lead to holiness of heart and life.

Holiness of heart and life is the ultimate goal of the covenant and the weekly group meeting. Holiness is formed as disciples are encouraged through the weekly accountability and support for following Jesus' teachings, summarized by him in Matthew 22:37-40. When asked to define holiness Wesley quoted Philippians 2:5 and 1 John 2:6, "Having the mind that was in Christ, and walking just as he walked."

Identify the clauses that need to be adjusted or replaced. Select a member of the group to serve as scribe for the revision process. All members must agree to the parts of the covenant to be revised. All members must agree to the changes before they become part of the revised covenant.

One way to do the work of revision is to agree that the weekly meetings will include time to work out the changes that need to be made to fit the current and future development of the group. Keep in mind that the covenant's purpose is to prompt growth in holiness of heart and life that leads to disciples who help the church to make disciples. Agree that the first forty-five minutes of these meetings will be devoted to mutual accountability for discipleship. The remaining fifteen minutes are devoted to working out the revisions to the covenant.

This process requires that group members do some homework. First, each member needs to pray daily for the leading of the Holy Spirit in the work of revising the group's covenant. The entire process must be steeped in prayer and invoking the leading of the Holy Spirit. Second, members need to give prayerful thought to the changes they believe will best help themselves and the group to have the mind of Christ and to walk just as he walked. Take notes and bring the notes to the weekly meeting to be shared with the group.

Technology may be used to facilitate and speed the revision process. Social media like Facebook enhance conversation and sharing of ideas between meetings. Google Docs and Dropbox are other helpful tools that enable the group to edit and add their ideas to covenant revision.

After the desired changes are made to everyone's satisfaction the revised covenant is then signed. Copies are made and distributed to the group members and to the pastor. You may want to invite the pastor to attend the meeting when the new covenant is signed and ask him or her to serve the Eucharist as a way of ratifying the covenant.

The covenant shared by a Covenant Discipleship group is a living document. As the group grows and matures in holiness of heart and life, the covenant needs to help the growth to continue. If your group has been living with a covenant for more than a year, it may be time for the group to evaluate and revise it. The beginning of a new year is an excellent time to recommit, renew, or revise your group's covenant.

APPENDIX D

Leading a Covenant Discipleship Group Meeting

Leading the weekly Covenant Discipleship group meeting is an important skill to learn. One unique characteristic of Covenant Discipleship groups is shared leadership. Everyone takes turns leading the meetings from week to week. This is one way group members are formed as leaders in discipleship who help the congregation live out its mission to make disciples of Jesus Christ for the transformation of the world. Shared leadership also means that the weekly meeting experience is shaped by the personality and style of that week's leader.

The main job of the leader is to manage the time and the conversation. Managing the time means beginning and ending on time. The group meets for one hour. The leader directs the conversation guided by the group's covenant. He ensures that everyone has time to give an account of the week. He makes sure no one member monopolizes the time.

During the accountability time the leader always begins with her account of each clause of the covenant. She reads the clause aloud and then gives her account of what she did or failed to do since the last meeting.

The best way of giving your account is by telling stories. They are an effective way of building up the group and helping members

who may be struggling with parts of the covenant. Stories often provide ideas about practices that others may adapt for themselves. As
you give your account, it's important that as the leader you give an
example to others in the group by exercising brevity. Get to the point
quickly, conclude, and move on to the next person. The leader, and
others in the group, may ask questions. The leader's task is to manage the covenant conversation so the meeting is concluded as close to
the hour as possible.

Here is a suggested agenda for a Covenant Discipleship group
meeting:

Prayer (5 minutes)

The leader prepares a prayer invoking the presence of the
Holy Spirit to lead group members and the congregation
as channels of God's mission in the world. A hymn, hymn
stanza, or praise chorus may be sung.

Covenant accountability (50 minutes)

The leader leads the group in reading the covenant preamble
in unison. The leader selects a clause and gives her account
of her practice since the last meeting. The leader then calls
on each member of the group in turn to give an account of
his practice of that part of the covenant. The leader may ask
probing questions aimed at helping the person clarify his
account. Other members of the group may also ask questions aimed at helping the member clarify his account and to
encourage him. When all members have given their accounts
of their practice of that part of the covenant, the leader moves
on to the next clause. This process is repeated with each covenant clause.

Closing and prayer (5 minutes)

The leader concludes with words of encouragement for the
group. Ask who plans to attend next week and announce
who will lead next week. Conclude the meeting with sharing

prayer concerns, singing a couple of stanzas of a hymn, and praying a closing prayer with dismissal and blessing.

Groups may also include a brief version of the Lord's Supper. An ordained elder must preside at the table. If none are members of the group, then the group may invite the pastor of the congregation to join them at the end of the meeting.

Meetings are one hour. Be sure to begin and end on time. Do not delay the meeting time for persons who arrive late.

Meetings may be held anywhere the group can have an undisturbed, private conversation. Groups may meet at the church, member homes, or an office building where one or more members work. Meeting at a restaurant or other public space could work if the group can reserve a private room.

Do not serve food during meetings. If you want to share a meal, then plan to serve the food after the group completes its hour of accountability for their mutual covenant. Do not let the food distract you from the group's mission to "watch over one another in love" and to help one another become more faithful, dependable disciples of Jesus Christ.

The meeting day, time, and location must be published in the church calendar. This reminds group members and the congregation that the groups are part of the congregation's mission to make disciples of Jesus Christ who join in his transformational work in the world. Remember, the group is as much for the benefit of the congregation as it is a blessing to each member. The mission of Covenant Discipleship groups is to form members as disciples who make disciples; they are leaders in discipleship the congregation needs for its mission to make disciples of Jesus Christ for the transformation of the world.

Use social media such as Skype, Google Hangouts, and FaceTime only when one or more group members cannot get to the meeting room. Christianity is an incarnational faith. God put on flesh and blood and became one of us in Jesus Christ. Eugene Peterson, in his translation of John 1:14 (The Message), describes the incarnation

of God: "The Word became flesh and blood, and moved into the
neighborhood." In other words, in Jesus, God came physically to
show us the way, the truth, and the life. People could see, hear, touch,
and smell Jesus. He reached out and touched women and men to
heal them. He embraced children. His arms outstretched on the cross
embraced the whole world with God's love and justice. All this is
to make the point that Christians are formed when we meet face to
face, when we can reach out to touch and even smell one another. We
lose something important when we try to substitute digital images
and sounds on screen and through speakers. Use social media, but
use it sparingly when it is the only alternative to the physical presence
of a group member in the meeting.

APPENDIX E

The "Doldrums"*: What To Do When Your Group Becomes Boring

*"a spell of listlessness or despondency"

By David Lowes Watson

(Reprinted from *Covenant Discipleship: Christian Formation through Mutual Accountability*, pp. 163–64. Used by permission.)

The catechesis of being accountable for aspects of discipleship which have been neglected or taken for granted, gives each group a wealth of insight and challenge during the first two months of meeting together. After three or four months, however, a sense of routine sets in. The questions seem to become mechanical. Answers lack spontaneity, and members begin to question the validity and usefulness of the whole exercise.

It should be clearly stated to new groups that this time of "doldrums" is to be expected, and for two reasons. The most immediate cause is the wish to turn to something new when the novelty of the groups has worn off. In part this is reflective of our culture's preoccupation with self-fulfillment, and it should be firmly resisted. Indeed, withdrawing from religious "junk food" is one of the most important functions of covenant discipleship groups.

There is a deeper spiritual reason for the "doldrums," however, which can best be described as "getting a second wind." Most churchgoers today are out of practice when it comes to accountable discipleship. Many have allowed themselves to become spectators in church, watching and perhaps admiring those who seem to be committed to their faith, though not really wishing to join them in the work of Jesus Christ. Now that they are in a covenant discipleship group, there is no avoiding the challenge of discipleship. While this is exhilarating at first, there comes a time when the routine of the task begins to take hold, and when the daily grind requires stamina.

As a group gets this second wind, it should be explained that this is exactly what covenant discipleship is all about. It is an agreement to watch over one another in love. We are in covenant, not merely to share the high points in our journey, important though these are, but much more to sustain and support each other in the midst of the routine and the commonplace.

If a group remains faithful to its covenant through these "doldrums," it is not long before the rough and tumble of living in the world brings the member to realize even more profoundly the value of this common bond. Such times of apparent aimlessness are no more than a test of the commitment they have made, a searching and tempering of discipleship, a moving away from self-serving interests to those which are Christ-serving. It is a form of spiritual growth well attested in the history of the Christian faith; but groups need to know about it at the outset, and to be ready for it.

APPENDIX F

Bringing New Members into a Covenant Discipleship Group

Covenant Discipleship groups are open to everyone who is willing to be intentional and accountable for his or her discipleship. If your group has fewer than seven members, then you have room for new people. They may have recently joined the church and learned about the Covenant Discipleship groups. They may have been thinking and praying about joining a group but were not ready when the current groups were formed. Or a person may have had a recent experience in which the Holy Spirit prompted him or her to join fellow disciples to go deeper.

Covenant Discipleship groups need to remember that they exist to help the congregation live out its mission to make disciples of Jesus Christ for the transformation of the world. They do not exist primarily for the personal benefit of group members. This means that all Covenant Discipleship groups with fewer than seven members should be willing to receive new members. New members must be added with great care by following a simple process that respects the group process and the needs of the new person.

First, everyone in the group needs to agree to the addition of a new member. If there is no consensus, then the group needs to work through why one or more members are reluctant to welcome a new member. This is a good time to remind members of the group's mission: their primary purpose is to form leaders in discipleship who help the congregation to be faithful to its mission of making disciples of Jesus Christ.

Give the prospective member a copy of the group's covenant. Allow time for them to read and study it. Explain that they need to accept the covenant as it is. The group should not revise its covenant when a new member joins.

Explain to the prospective member that he or she is welcome to sit in on meetings for three weeks. He or she may simply attend as an observer or jump in and participate in the process of accountability with the covenant as the agenda. In my experience, prospective members tend to want to jump in with both feet and fully participate in the meetings. Ensure that prospective members understand the importance of confidentiality. Everything shared in the group meeting stays in the group.

Finally, at the conclusion of the third meeting, the prospective member needs to inform the group of his or her decision. The three meetings are sufficient to give the person a clear understanding of the group's nature and mission. If the person decides to stay, then he or she becomes a member of the group and is asked to sign the group's covenant. The covenant should not change when a new person joins a group. The new person will participate in covenant revision when the group decides it is time to do so.

If prospective members decide that Covenant Discipleship is not for them, then the group prays for them and tells them they will continue to pray that the Holy Spirit leads them to a group that meets their needs.

This is a simple and effective process that works well. It respects the integrity of existing groups and the needs of prospective members. It also reminds groups of their mission to help the congregation be faithful to its mission of making disciples of Jesus Christ for the transformation of the world.

APPENDIX G

Covenant Discipleship Groups and Social Media

If you have access to a high-speed network and a computer equipped with a camera and speakers then you have the power to participate in a small group meeting without leaving your home or office. By all means use the internet. But only under certain circumstances.

It is appropriate for groups to meet using the social media in these two circumstances:

- If some group members are out of town and physically separated from the group
- If a group member is confined to his or her home due to illness or is caring for a family member

Notice that both of these situations are temporary. The use of digital meeting applications to bring members into a meeting should be employed only when members are not able to participate in the group meeting in person.

Google Hangouts, Skype, and FaceTime are great tools, but they should not be used as a substitute for physical meetings when physical meetings are possible. An important part of mutual support and accountability for discipleship is the routine of getting yourself to the meeting and being physically present to group members. The effort needed to get yourself to a meeting and then the work of listening and participating with the group keeps you mindful that you are an embodied spirit.

John Wesley was fond of saying, "The soul and body make a *person*. The Spirit and discipline make a Christian" (see Sermon 122, "Causes of the Inefficacy of Christianity, ¶7). Part of our discipline is the act of meeting face to face with fellow pilgrims who are striving to move toward holiness of heart and life. An essential part of discipleship formation is being physically present to others; being able to see, hear, smell, and touch one another is just as important as weekly accountability for how we performed the works of mercy and works of piety stated in the group covenant.

The digital meeting tools available to us are great for bringing group members into a meeting. But virtual presence is no substitute for real presence. The various applications must not be used as a regular substitute for physical meetings.

APPENDIX H

Group Dynamics

A frequently asked question in my Covenant Discipleship workshop goes something like this: "What do you do when someone in the group consistently talks so much that everyone cannot give their account of the covenant within the hour meeting time?"

I have a few suggestions for this common problem. The first is that the leader can assert his or her role by reminding group members to give their account of the covenant in a way that everyone gets a turn and every clause is covered within the hour.

Second, suggest a three-minute limit for each person's account of each covenant clause. The leader keeps track of the time. When a member gets close to the three-minute mark, the leader gives a gentle prompt to wrap up and move on to the next person.

Third, if the person or persons cannot keep within the three minutes, then the group could adopt the use of a three-minute sand timer. Get a timer for each person. Each member turns the timer over at the beginning of his or her account of each covenant clause. All agree to complete their account of each covenant clause before all the sand falls to the bottom of the timer.

Finally, if the problem persists, remind everyone of the group's mission to help each other to grow in holiness of heart and life through mutual accountability. The focus of the group is discipleship.

The covenant is the agenda. Each person gives his or her account of each clause of the covenant in a way that builds up the group. The point is to build up the group, not to build up your own ego. That's why it's important that everyone has an opportunity to share about each clause of the covenant within the hour meeting time.

Certainly there will be times in every group when one or more members need extra time to share their experience, to vent, or to process feelings with the group. Over time members grow in trust and love for one another. I'm not saying that members must always be disciplined in their weekly meetings. However, I am saying that such times should be the exception and not the rule of the group meeting. The way to handle a member's need for lengthy sharing is to suggest one or more members meet with him or her after the group meeting to listen and to pray with him or her.

If the group fails to be clear about its mission to help each other grow in discipleship shaped by the group's covenant and the General Rule of Discipleship, then it will inevitably shift into a sharing or fellowship group. In other words, if we are not careful to keep Christ at the center of our meeting and our conversation, then we will inevitably replace him with ourselves. The group then shifts to focusing upon personal growth and blessing of members rather than the mission of the church (to make disciples of Jesus Christ for the transformation of the world).

If you have group members who dominate the meeting time, then remember the word of the apostle Paul to speak "the truth in love, we must grow up . . . into Christ, from whom the whole body, joined and knit together by every ligament with which it is equipped, as each part is working properly, promotes the body's growth in building itself up in love" (Eph. 4:15-16).

APPENDIX I

A Love Feast for Covenant Discipleship Groups

The following introduction was adapted from the article "A Love Feast for Covenant Discipleship Groups" (Covenant Discipleship Quarterly, *Spring 2000), by Dean McIntyre, former Music Resources Director, Discipleship Ministries.*

The Love Feast was, for many years, an important part of life in the Methodist societies. John Wesley adapted it from the Moravian Agape Meal. It was an informal time of prayer, singing, testimony, and sharing of food and water. The Love Feast was held monthly for society members. Methodists looked forward to the monthly event.

The United Methodist Book of Worship contains historical information about the Love Feast, suggestions for its use, listings of appropriate hymns and scriptures, and the service itself (pp. 581–84). Given the time constraints of the Covenant Discipleship group meeting, it is impossible to use the full service at a weekly meeting. What follows is an abbreviated order, which contains some elements and preserves the form of the *Book of Worship* service while making use of elements from other forms of the Love Feast.

The Love Feast may serve as an order for a weekly meeting. The reading of the covenant and each person's time of accountability serve to replace the "Address or Personal Witness to the Scripture" and the "Testimonies, Prayers, Singing" portions of the Love Feast in the *Book of Worship*.

When using the Love Feast, the leader should distribute copies to each member present. Permission is granted for you to use and adapt the order below in your Covenant Discipleship group, inserting your group's covenant.

Because some persons may see similarities between the Love Feast and Holy Communion, it is good to make clear to them that this is not the sacrament at which an ordained elder presides but is a simple sharing of food led by a layperson.

BRIEF ORDER FOR A LOVE FEAST FOR COVENANT DISCIPLESHIP GROUPS

HYMN
Tune: TERRA BEATA (144) or DIADEMATA (327), *The United Methodist Hymnal*
Text: Charles Wesley

> Father of earth and heaven,
> Thy hungry children feed,
> Thy grace be to our spirits given,
> That true immortal bread.
> Grant us and all our race
> In Jesus Christ to prove
> The sweetness of thy pardoning grace,
> The manna of your love.

SCRIPTURE
Suggested readings:
Psalm 145:8-21
Luke 9:12-17
Luke 10:25-37

Luke 14:16-24
John 6:25-35
John 15:1-17
1 Corinthians 13
2 Corinthians 9:6-15
Philippians 2:5-11
1 John 4:7-21
Matthew 22:34-40

PRAYERS
This prayer from John Wesley or others may be offered by the leader and group members.

> O God, seeing there is in Christ Jesus
>   an infinite fullness of all that we can want or desire,
> O that we may all receive of his fullness, grace upon grace;
>   grace to pardon our sins, and subdue our iniquities;
>   to justify our persons and to sanctify our souls;
> and to complete that holy change, that renewal of our hearts,
>   whereby we may be transformed
>   into that blessed image wherein you did create us.
> O make us all acceptable to be partakers
>   of the inheritance of your saints in light. Amen.

OUR COVENANT
Here the group reads its covenant together and each person gives account of her or his discipleship.

LORD'S PRAYER

FELLOWSHIP OF EATING AND PASSING THE CUP
As group members pass bread, cake, crackers, or other food to their neighbor they say:
God loves you, and there's nothing you can do about it.

HYMN or DOXOLOGY
Suggestions:

UMH 186	Alleluia	TFWS 2223	They'll Know We Are Christians by Our Love
UMH 659	Jesus Our Friend and Brother	TFWS 2222	The Servant Song
UMH 665	Go Now in Peace	TFWS 2226	Bind Us Together
UMH 432	Jesu, Jesu	TFWS 2224	Make Us One
UMH 583	Sois la Semilla (You Are the Seed)	TFWS 2233	Where Children Belong
UMH 572	Pass It On	TFWS 2168	Love the Lord Your God
UMH 566	Blest Be the Dear Uniting Love	TFWS 2167	More Like You
UMH 560	Help Us Accept Each Other	TFWS 2171	Make Me a Channel of Your Peace
UMH 389	Freely, Freely	TFWS 2175	Together We Serve
UMH 402	Lord, I Want to Be a Christian	TFWS 2176	Make Me a Servant
UMH 422	Jesus, Thine All-Victorious Love	TFWS 2179	Live in Charity
UMH 94	Praise God . . .	TFWS 2040	Awesome God

DISMISSAL

(*All may pray the Covenant Prayer in the Wesleyan Tradition, UMH 607*)

> I am no longer my own, but thine.
> Put me to what thou wilt, rank me with whom thou wilt.
> Put me to doing, put me to suffering.
> Let me be employed by thee or laid aside for thee,
> exalted for thee or brought low for thee.
> Let me be full, let me be empty.
> Let me have all things, let me have nothing.
> I freely and heartily yield all things
> to thy pleasure and disposal.
> And now, O glorious and blessed God,
> Father, Son, and Holy Spirit,
> thou art mine, and I am thine. So be it.
> And the covenant which I have made on earth,
> let it be ratified in heaven. Amen.

Sources: *UM Book of Worship, UM Hymnal, Methodism and the Love-Feast* by Frank Baker (New York: Macmillan, 1957).

APPENDIX J

A Service of Dedication for Covenant Discipleship Groups

By Rev. Taylor Burton-Edwards, Director of
Worship Resources, Discipleship Ministries

THE ORDER OF SERVICE

As an act of response to the Word, the pastor invites members of Covenant Discipleship groups or other groups guided by the General Rule of Discipleship to gather around the font in their groups. When all have arrived, the pastor addresses the congregation (the groups' and congregation's responses are in bold type):

Sisters and brothers in Christ,
   through the Sacrament of Baptism
   we are initiated into Christ's holy church.
We are incorporated into Christ's mighty acts of salvation
   and given new birth through water and the Spirit
All this is God's gift, offered without price.
Through coming together in disciplined groups,
   watching over one another in love,
      we help each other live out our baptismal vows
         and our General Rules
as expressed in the General Rule of Discipleship:

To witness to Jesus Christ in the world,
    and to follow his teachings through
        acts of compassion, justice, worship, and devotion,
under the guidance of the Holy Spirit.

These groups present themselves today
    to share their commitments to God,
        to each other and to you as members with you
        in this congregation of Christ's holy church.
They ask for your prayers and your blessing.

Pastor to the groups:
How do you pledge to witness to Jesus Christ in the world
and to follow his teachings through acts of compassion?
    Each group reads aloud its covenant for acts of compassion.
How do you pledge to witness to Jesus Christ in the world
and to follow his teachings through acts of justice?
    Each group reads aloud its covenant for acts of justice.
How do you pledge to witness to Jesus Christ in the world
and to follow his teachings through acts of devotion?
    Each group reads aloud its covenant for acts of devotion.
How do you pledge to witness to Jesus Christ in the world
and to follow his teachings through acts of worship?
    Each group reads aloud its covenant for acts of worship.

Pastor to congregation:
Let us extend our hands in blessing
    toward these sisters and brothers,
        and the commitments they make before God
        and this congregation.
Let us pray:
Almighty God,
    we thank you for the living witness
    of sisters and brothers who are pledging to follow Christ
    and witness to his teachings in the world.

Pour out your Spirit on them.
Come, Holy Spirit.

Pour out your Spirit on us.
Come, Holy Spirit.

Give them the strength
to keep the commitments they have made to you
and to each other.

Give us the love and the wisdom
to support their growth in holiness
all the days of their lives.

Through Jesus Christ our Lord,
    to whom be blessing and honor,
    glory and power, wisdom and strength,
now and forever. **Amen.**

Covenant Discipleship Groups may lead the exchange of peace with
these or other words:
The peace of our Lord Jesus Christ be always with you.
And also with you.

APPENDIX K

An Order for the Commissioning of Class Leaders

(*The United Methodist Book of Worship*, p. 602)

This order is intended for the public commissioning of class leaders following their appointment by a charge or church conference of the congregation.

The order may be led by the pastor of the congregation, the district superintendent, or the bishop of the area.

As a Response to the Word, or at some other appropriate place within a service of congregational worship, the pastor invites the newly appointed class leader(s) to come forward.

Pastor to congregation:

Dear friends, the office of class leader is one of the most important contributions made by world Methodism to the pastoral leadership of Christ's holy Church.

In the General Rules of 1743, John Wesley described the Methodist societies as companies of men and women who, "having the form, and seeking the power of godliness," came together in order to pray, to receive the word of exhortation and "to watch over one another in love that they may help each other work out their salvation." To this end, the societies were divided into small companies, called classes, each with an appointed leader "to advise, reprove, comfort, and exhort, as occasion may require."

Class leaders of today continue this tradition. In the founding Discipline of our church, they are described as persons "not only of sound judgment, but truly devoted to God," who are willing to help others in the congregation "to grow in the knowledge and love of God."

Pastor to class leader(s):

Do you accept the office of class leader in this congregation of The United Methodist Church?

I do.

Will you exercise this office by helping other members of the congregation to fulfill the general rule of discipleship: To witness to Jesus Christ in the world and to follow his teachings through acts of compassion, justice, worship, and devotion under the guidance of the Holy Spirit.

I will.

Will you help other members of the congregation to fulfill the general rule of discipleship, not by judging them, but by watching over them in love?

I will.

Will you meet weekly in covenant with others of like mind and purpose to be accountable for your own discipleship?

I will.

Pastor to congregation:

Will you affirm the call of these men and women to be class leaders in this congregation of The United Methodist Church?

We will.

Will you acknowledge them as your leaders in discipleship, and accept their guidance as they watch over you in love?

We will.

Pastor to class leader(s):

You are hereby commissioned as class leaders in this congregation of The United Methodist Church.

Let us pray.

Most gracious God, bless your servant(s) whom we now entrust with the office of class leader. Grant them wisdom tempered by your love, and courage tempered by your justice, so that Jesus Christ might be honored and served by all in this congregation, to the furtherance of your coming reign, on earth as in heaven; through the same Jesus Christ our Lord. Amen.

UMH 438, "Forth in Thy Name, O Lord," may then be sung.

NOTES

Introduction

1. *The Book of Discipline of The United Methodist Church 2012* (Nashville: The United Methodist Publishing House, 2013), ¶120.

2. Marjorie Thompson, *Soul Feast: An Invitation to the Christian Spiritual Life* (Louisville: Westminster John Knox, 1995), p. 138.

3. The General Rules of the Methodist Church, *The United Methodist Book of Discipline 2012*, ¶104, (Nashville: The United Methodist Publishing House, 2013), pp. 75–78.

4. *The United Methodist Hymnal* (Nashville: United Methodist Publishing House, 1989), p. 34. Discussion of the baptismal covenant can be found on pages 33–39.

5. *The United Methodist Hymnal: Book of United Methodist Worship*, "Prayer of Confession," Word & Table I (Nashville: The United Methodist Publishing House, 1989), p. 8.

6. *The Interpreter's Dictionary of the Bible*, vol. 1, s.v. "disciple."

7. John Wesley, Sermon 89, "The More Excellent Way," ¶5, in *Sermons III*, ed. Albert C. Outler, vol. 3 of *The Bicentennial Edition of the Works of John Wesley* (Nashville: Abingdon, 1976–), p. 265.

8. Ibid., p. 266.

9. *Book of Discipline 2012*, ¶120.

10. Ibid., ¶1117.2.

11. John Wesley, Hymn 489:3–4, in *A Collection of Hymns for the Use of the People Called Methodists*, ed. Franz Hildebrandt and Oliver A. Beckerlegge, vol. 7 of *Bicentennial Edition*, p. 677.

12. "A Collect for Peace," in Morning Prayer II, *The Book of Common Prayer* (New York: Seabury Press, 1979), p. 99.

13. John Wesley's phrase "holiness of heart and life" cited here is found in "Advice to the People Called Methodists," ¶2, in *The Methodist Societies: History, Nature, and Design*, ed. Rupert E. Davies, vol. 9 of *The Bicentennial Edition of the Works of John Wesley* (Nashville: Abingdon Press, 1976–), 123–24. John Wesley's phrase "to have the mind of Christ and to walk just as he walked" combines Philippians 2:5 and 1 John 2:6.

14. *United Methodist Hymnal*, 607.

Chapter 1

1. For more on this topic, please read chapter 2 of David Lowes Watson, *Forming Christian Disciples: The Role of Covenant Discipleship and Class Leaders in the Congregation* published by Wipf and Stock.

2. *The United Methodist Hymnal*, "Commendation and Welcome," p. 38.

3. General Rule of Discipleship, *The Book of Discipline of The United Methodist Church 2012* (Nashville: Abingdon, 2009), ¶1117.2a.

4. Mike Breen, *Building a Discipling Church*, Kindle ed. (Kindle Locations 100–101, 2011). 3DM.

5. *The United Methodist Book of Discipline 2012*, ¶104 (Nashville: The United Methodist Publishing House, 2013), pp. 75–78.

6. Charles Wesley, "The Poor as Jesus' Bosom-Friends," in *Songs for the Poor*, ed. S T Kimbrough Jr. (New York: General Board of Global Ministries, 1997), hymn 3.

7. John Wesley, "Advice to the People Called Methodists," ¶2, in *The Methodist Societies: History, Nature, and Design*, ed. Rupert E. Davies, vol. 9 of *Bicentennial Edition*, pp. 123–24.

8. John Wesley, Sermon 92, "On Zeal," §II.5, in *Sermons III, Bicentennial Edition.*

9. "Baptismal Covenant I," p. 35.

Chapter 2

1. "Baptismal Covenant I," pp. 34–35.

2. Wesley, preface to *Hymns and Sacred Poems* (Oxford: 1739), p. viii.

3. John Wesley, April 2, 1739, *Journals and Diaries II (1738–1743)*, ed. W. Reginald Ward and Richard P. Heitzenrater, vol. 19 of *The Bicentennial Edition of The Works of John Wesley* (Nashville: Abingdon Press, 1976—), p. 46.

4. *The United Methodist Hymnal,* "Baptismal Covenant I," p. 34.

5. For more on the Methodist class meeting, please see David Lowes Watson, *The Early Methodist Class Meeting: Its Origins and Significance* published by Wipf and Stock.

6. Wesley, Hymn 507.3–4, *Works,* p. 7:698.

7. Wesley, Sermon 16, "The Means of Grace," §II.1, *Works,* p. 1:381.

8. Wesley, Sermon 85, "On Working Out Our Own Salvation," § III.7, *Works,* pp. 3:208–9.

9. John Wesley, *A Plain Account of Christian Perfection* (London: Epworth, 1952), p. 100.

10. John Wesley, Sermon 16, "The Means of Grace," §III.1, *Works,* p. 1:384.

11. Ibid., §III.7–10, p. 1:386–89.

12. Ibid., §III.12, pp. 1:389–90.

13. John Wesley, Sermon 92, "On Zeal," §II.9, *Works,* p. 3:314.

14. Ibid.

15. *The United Methodist Hymnal,* rubric 4 "Renunciation of Sin and Profession of Faith," p. 34.

16. David Lowes Watson, *Forming Christian Disciples: The Role of Covenant Discipleship and Class Leaders in the Congregation* (Nashville: Discipleship Resources, 1991), p. 52.

17. Charles Wesley, *The United Methodist Hymnal,* hymn 385.

Chapter 3

1. "The General Rules of The Methodist Church," ¶104, *The Book of Discipline of The United Methodist Church 2012*, p. 76.

2. Wesley, Advice to the People Called Methodists, ¶2, *Works*, 9:123.

3. *Acedia* is a Latin term meaning a state of restlessness and inability either to work or to pray.

4. Catechesis is historically the process of religious instruction preparing persons for baptism. Persons desiring to become Christians are taught the doctrines and practices of the church and the Christian life.

5. Roberta C. Bondi, *To Love as God Loves: Conversations with the Early Church* (Philadelphia: Fortress Press, 1987), p. 25.

Chapter 4

1. Wesley, Sermon 45, "The New Birth," §II.4, *Works*, 2:193.

2. Wesley, Sermon 92, "On Zeal," §II.8–9, *Works*, 3:314.

3. *The United Methodist Hymnal*, Baptismal Covenant I, rubric 6: "According to the grace given you, will you remain *faithful members* of Christ's holy church and serve as Christ's *representatives* in the world? **I will**," p. 34, emphasis added.

4. Ibid.

5. John Wesley, Advice to the People Called Methodists, ¶2, in *The Methodist Societies: History, Nature, and Design*, ed. Rupert E. Davies, vol. 9 of *The Bicentennial Edition of The Works of John Wesley* (Nashville: Abingdon Press, 1976—), 123.

Chapter 5

1. *The United Methodist Hymnal*, "Baptismal Covenant I:8," p. 35.

2. Breen, *Building a Discipling Culture*, 3DM.

3. Ibid.

4. *The United Methodist Hymnal*, "Baptismal Covenant IV," pp. 50–53.

5. This is a phrase used frequently by John Wesley as shorthand for describing the goal of the Christian life.

Chapter 6

1. To learn about the importance of the class meeting and class leaders read David Lowes Watson, *The Early Methodist Class Meeting: Its Origins and Significance* and *Class Leaders: Recovering a Tradition* published by Wipf and Stock.

2. *The Book of Discipline of The United Methodist Church 2012*, ¶104.

3. See "Baptismal Covenant I," p. 34.

4. Ibid., p. 38.

5. Wesley, Hymn 489, *Works*, pp. 7:676–77.

6. See *The United Methodist Book of Worship* (Nashville: Abingdon, 1992), pp. 602–4.

7. David Lowes Watson, *Class Leaders: Recovering a Tradition* (Eugene, OR: Wipf and Stock, 1998), p. 72.

8. "To serve the present age, my calling to fulfill; O may it all my powers engage to do my Master's will!" See stanza 2 of "A Charge to Keep I Have," in *The United Methodist Hymnal*, hymn 413.

9. "A rule of life is a pattern of spiritual disciplines that provides structure and direction for growth in holiness. . . . It fosters gifts of the Spirit in personal life and human community, helping to form us into the persons God intends us to be." Thompson, *Soul Feast*, p. 138.

10. Watson, *Class Leaders*, p. 72.

11. Ibid.

12. Ibid.

13. Ibid., pp. 74–75.

14. "Baptismal Covenant I," p. 35.

15. Ibid.

16. Watson, *Class Leaders*, p. 127.

17. Watson, *Class Leaders*, p. 134.

18. Ibid.

19. Wesley, Advice to the People Called Methodists, ¶2, *Works*, 9:123.

20. Watson, *Class Leaders*, p. 91.

Chapter 7

1. Numerous quotations in this section are from the work of David Lowes Watson and the groundbreaking work he did at the General Board of Discipleship to develop and establish Covenant Discipleship groups and class leaders as a means for The United Methodist Church to re-tradition the office of class leaders and classes for the contemporary church.

2. "A rule of life is a pattern of spiritual disciplines that provide structure and direction for growth in holiness. . . . It fosters gifts of the Spirit in personal life and human community, helping to form us into the persons God intends us to be." Thompson, *Soul Feast*, p. 138.

3. Wesley, Sermon 24, "Upon Our Lord's Sermon on the Mount, IV," §I.1, *Works*, pp. 1:533–34.

4. Watson, *Forming Christian Disciples*, p. 142.

5. Ibid., p. 143.

6. Wesley, Advice to the People Called Methodists, ¶2, *Works*, 9:123.

7. Watson, *Forming Christian Disciples*, p. 145.

8. Ibid., p. 146.

9. Ibid.

10. Ibid., p. 147.

11. Ibid., p. 149.

12. Ibid.

13. Ibid., p. 150.

14. Ibid., p. 156.

15. Ibid., pp. 157–58.

16. Ibid., pp. 158–67.

17. *The United Methodist Hymnal*, Baptismal Covenant I, page 35.

Epilogue

1. Wesley, Sermon 92, On Zeal, §II.5 & 6, *Works*, 3:313, emphasis added.

2. *The United Methodist Hymnal*, Baptismal Covenant I, p. 35.

3. David Lowes Watson, *Forming Christian Disciples: The Role of Covenant Discipleship and Class Leaders in the Congregation*, p. 24.

4. *The United Methodist Hymnal*, 561:2, 4.

COVENANT DISCIPLESHIP LEXICON

the General Rule of Discipleship. "To witness to Jesus Christ in the world, and to follow his teachings through acts of compassion, justice, worship, and devotion under the guidance of the Holy Spirit." This General Rule is the foundation of Covenant Discipleship groups. It is derived from the General Rules. Both are found in *The Book of Discipline of The United Methodist Church.*

balanced discipleship. The General Rule of Discipleship helps Covenant Discipleship groups maintain balance between all the teachings of Jesus and mitigates against focusing only on those persons are temperamentally inclined toward. The General Rule helps persons to practice both works of piety (acts of worship and acts of devotion) *and* works of mercy (acts of compassion and acts of justice). It also guides persons to attend to the personal dimensions of discipleship (acts of compassion and acts of devotion) *and* the public (acts of justice and acts of worship). The General Rule of Discipleship is inclusive and practicable.

witness. A witness testifies to the truth. A witness has personal experience with a person or event. The experience of witnesses enables them to tell others about the one they know. Christians are baptized, called, and equipped to witness to Jesus Christ in the world. We witness to what Jesus witnessed to: the reign of God that is breaking out in the world and that is coming.

Jesus' teachings. Jesus summarized his teachings in Matthew 22:37-40: " 'You shall love the Lord your God with all your heart, and with all your soul, and with all your mind.' This is the greatest and first commandment. And a second is like it: 'You shall love your neighbor as yourself.' On these two commandments hang all the law and the prophets." The General Rule of Discipleship and the covenant that each Covenant Discipleship group writes are intended to help Christians obey Jesus' teachings.

acts of compassion. The simple acts of kindness we do for another person. For example, when we meet someone who is hungry, the act of compassion is to give him or her something to eat.

acts of justice. The actions Christians participate in with others, as communities of faith, to address the systemic and institutional causes of our neighbor's suffering. Christ calls us not only to help a person who is suffering but also to ask why the person is suffering and then to act to address the causes of injustice.

acts of worship. What Christians do together to offer themselves in service to God through praise, prayer, hymn, confession, forgiveness, scripture, proclamation, and sacrament.

acts of devotion. The practices Christians do alone to nurture and participate in their personal relationship with God: daily prayer and Bible reading, centering prayer, keeping a journal, intercessory prayer, devotional reading, writing, and fasting or abstinence.

covenant. Each Covenant Discipleship group writes a covenant shaped by the General Rule of Discipleship. The covenant serves as the agenda for the weekly meeting. It has three essential parts: preamble, a list of up to ten clauses, and a conclusion. The preamble is a shared statement of the group's shared faith in Christ and the purpose of the covenant. The clauses are balanced between acts of compassion, justice, worship, and devotion and appear in the same order in which the practices are named in the General Rule of Discipleship. The conclusion is a brief statement reaffirming the nature of the covenant and group members' shared dependence upon grace to live the Christian life.

accountability. Covenant Discipleship groups are accountability groups. They meet weekly for one hour for mutual accountability and support for discipleship guided by the covenant they have written and shaped by the General Rule of Discipleship. Accountability practiced in these groups is simply each member giving an account of what he or she has done, or not done, in light of the group's covenant. It is telling stories about how the group member has lived the Christian life since the last meeting, guided by the group's covenant. The leader, and other group members, can ask questions. The purpose of accountability is to "watch over one another in love" and to help one another grow and mature in holiness of heart and life; loving God with all our heart, soul, and mind, and loving those whom God loves, as God loves them.

weekly meetings. Covenant Discipleship groups meet weekly for one hour. Experience tells us that the weekly meeting is essential. It is the best way for the group to help one another grow in discipleship through accountability and support. Children's Covenant Discipleship groups meet for one and a half to two hours each week to accommodate acts of compassion and justice.

BIBLIOGRAPHY

Carder, Kenneth L. *The United Methodist Way: Living Our Beliefs*, rev. ed. Nashville: Disicpleship Resources, 2009.

Carder, Kenneth L., and Lacey C. Warner. *Grace to Lead: Practicing Leadership in the Wesleyan Tradition*. Nashville: General Board of Higher Education and Ministry, 2011.

Kisker, Scott. *Mainline or Methodist? Rediscovering Our Evangelistic Mission*. Nashville: Discipleship Resources, 2008.

Manskar, Steven W. *Accountable Discipleship: Living in God's Household*. Nashville: Discipleship Resources, 1999.

Manskar, Steven W., Diana Hynson, and Marjorie Suchocki. *A Perfect Love: Understanding John Wesley's "A Plain Account of Christian Perfection."* Nashville: Discipleship Resources, 2002.

Watson, David Lowes. *The Early Methodist Class Meeting*. Eugene, OR: Wipf and Stock, 2002.

———. *Class Leaders: Recovering a Tradition*. Eugene, OR: Wipf and Stock, 2002.

———. *Covenant Discipleship: Christian Formation through Mutual Accountability*. Eugene, OR: Wipf and Stock, 2002.

———. *Forming Christian Disciples: The Role of Covenant Discipleship and Class Leaders in the Congregation*. Eugene, OR: Wipf and Stock, 2002.

Watson, Kevin M. *A Blueprint for Discipleship: Wesley's General Rules as a Guide for Christian Living*. Nashville: Discipleship Resources, 2009.

CPSIA information can be obtained
at www.ICGtesting.com
Printed in the USA
LVOW08s1102070317
526326LV00004B/6/P